MIKE MOUNTAIN HORSE
MY PEOPLE THE BLOODS

With editing and Introduction by
HUGH A. DEMPSEY

GLENBOW-ALBERTA INSTITUTE
and
BLOOD TRIBAL COUNCIL
1979

Published 1979 by Glenbow-Alberta Institute
Calgary, Alberta, and
Blood Tribal Council
Standoff, Alberta

Published with the assistance of a grant
from the Alberta Indian Treaties Commemorative
Program, Government of Alberta.

ISBN-0-919224-03-2

Contents

Introduction

MIKE MOUNTAIN HORSE was a man ahead of his time. A scholar and historian during a period when most Blood Indians were still learning the rudiments of farming and ranching, he was an isolated man, set off from his comrades by his own literary talents. He was also frustrated, for his background and limited education confined him to laboring and menial jobs for his entire life.

Much of Mike Mountain Horse's story appears in bits and pieces in his own narrative. The son of Mountain Horse of the Blood tribe and Black Face of the Peigans, he came from two families of prominent leaders. His paternal uncle was Bull Shield, a minor chief of the Bloods, while his maternal grandfather was Crow Flag, a leading Peigan war chief.

Born in 1888, Mountain Horse had no direct knowledge of the buffalo days, yet throughout his childhood he heard the thrilling tales of warriors, battles, hunting expeditions, and supernatural events. According to his own recollections, at the age of six he was with some other boys who were caught putting railroad ties on the tracks near Whoop-Up and was sent to St. Paul's mission school adjacent to the Blood Reserve so he would be "kept out of mischief and get educated as well." At the turn of the century he was transferred to the Calgary

The author, Mike Mountain Horse, is seen at right with two fellow ex-pupils of the mission school in 1911. At centre is James Gladstone.

Indian Industrial School to learn the carpentry trade and a "clean and cultured life." At that time he was more interested in sports than literary pursuits, serving as captain of the soccer team and developing an active interest in foot racing. Upon graduation in 1905, he raced professionally for a time under the name of Mike Deerfoot, being matched against some of the leading western Canadian runners of the day.

As a child, he was given the name of Captured Three Guns; as a teenager he was called Eagle Flying; and as an adult he took his grandfather's name of Crow Flag. Yet to the white people he was always known, somewhat condescendingly as "The Chief."

After his graduation, he worked in various jobs near the Blood Reserve until he was engaged as scout for the Mounted Police at Kipp detachment in 1907. A year later, the responsibility for interpreting was added to his duties and he was transferred to Lethbridge. He went on routine patrols with the Mounted Police and also had the task of checking on the sick and elderly Indians in his district. During this time, he married Mary Taylor, the mixed-blood daughter of ex-whiskey trader Harry "Kamoose" Taylor.

In 1916, after his brother Albert died en route home after being gassed at Ypres, Mike joined the Canadian army as a private in the 191st battalion, reg. no. 895041, and served overseas in World War One. By the time he was discharged in 1918, he had reached the rank of acting sergeant and had been awarded the Distinguished Conduct Medal. He was an instructor of a machine gun squad, wounded twice in action, and on one occasion was buried alive for four days in the debris of a German trench. He was one of a handful of Bloods who offered themselves for military service and, for the remainder of his life, he was honoured by his tribe as a warrior.

Mike seldom lived on the Blood Reserve after he returned from France. He separated from his wife and was employed for the next 25 years for various detachments of the Mounted Police in the Lethbridge area. During this time, the principal of St. Paul's school, Canon S. H. Middleton, took an interest in him and was the first to encourage him to write.

It was while he was in Lethbridge that Mountain Horse began his serious writing and by the late 1920s, he was regularly submitting articles to the *Lethbridge Herald*. In 1933, he even resigned from his work with the Mounted Police to devote his full time to writing and lecturing. He visited schools throughout southern Alberta and into British Columbia, telling about Indian life, but there was not enough money from literary sources to support him, and he was obliged to return to his previous profession. During this period his work came to the attention of Thyrza Young Burkitt and, with her help, a book-length manuscript "Indians of the Western Plains" was completed in about 1936. A number of Lethbridge citizens tried to get the manuscript published, even enlisting the aid of a Miss Ridley in Toronto. However, Canada was in the depths of a Depression and had no interest in the life and culture of the Blood tribe. Eventually the manuscript was filed away and forgotten—even Mike Mountain Horse did not possess a copy during the latter part of his life. Only in recent years did a copy come to light in possession of lawyer A. B. Hogg, of Lethbridge, and is now published under the more appropriate title, *My People, the Bloods*.

In 1943, when working for the Mounted Police in Lethbridge, Mountain Horse accepted a job as locomotive labourer in the CPR shops in that city and remained there until his retirement ten years later. While thus employed, he served

Mike Mountain Horse in dancing costume, 1912

as president of the Lethbridge local of the Stationary Fireman, Oilers and Laborers Union.

The years away from the reserve were not happy ones for him. His failure to get his book published only added to the misery of a near-poverty existence, social ostracization and the resultant problems with alcohol. In later life, he was wed to Mary, a daughter of Joe Healy, from the Blood Reserve, and inherited a family of seven children by her two previous marriages. Mike had no children of his own, but the couple remained together until Mary's death in 1956.

Throughout his life, Mike was remembered primarily as a war veteran. He helped form an Indian war veterans association and was often invited to speak at schools and women's organizations. Yet because he preferred to live away from his reserve, he was often treated with suspicion by his fellow Bloods. One man described him as "kind of a simple guy" because he preferred writing and reading books.

Another informant said that "some of the people thought he was a windbag and used to laugh at him. He used to come home for the St. Paul's reunions and would make big talk and use big words, but no one took him seriously. As far as his writing was concerned, people knew he was writing for white people, but not many Indians read newspapers in those days. But the people never looked down on him, for they honoured him because he had gone to war."

After the death of his wife, Mountain Horse returned to the reserve to live and in 1959 he was elected to the Blood tribal council. His reputation as a war veteran superceded any petty criticism about writing or his marginal life in Lethbridge; the fact that he had been in battle was more important to the tribe. After serving a term in the council, Mountain Horse passed away on Feb. 2, 1964.

It is unfortunate that his manuscript was not published during Mountain Horse's lifetime, for it undoubtedly would have raised his stature both on and off his reserve. Not only is it a valuable document for the recollections of his own childhood experiences, but it also contains a wealth of primary information about the life and customs of his tribe.

The book, as published, contains a number of revisions. The first is the addition of two newspaper articles which were not included in the original volume. These include the opening chapter, "The Blood Tribe," from the June 19, 1937 edition of *Lethbridge Herald*, and "Tragedy at 18-Mile Lake," from the Sept. 26, 1931 issue of the same newspaper. Another revi-

The author often acted as master of ceremonies for native activities in Lethbridge. He is seen here, at right, in 1937 introducing Miss Nora Gladstone, a Blood girl who had just returned from the royal coronation in England. The others, left to right, are Cross Child, Lucy and Pauline Gladstone.

sion deals with content and style. When Mountain Horse wrote the manuscript in the 1930s, he was aiming for a non-Indian audience which he realized was prejudiced against the old-time pagan Indian. As a result, he tended to apologize for his own people's religious or warring practises, or hastened to assure the reader that things were different now that his people had become good Christians.

This writer knew Mike Mountain Horse well during the latter years of his life, for he married my wife's aunt. It was clear that Mike was a proud man and, although he considered himself to be a member of the Salvation Army, he also supported the beliefs and practises of his tribe. His negative comments in the manuscript were not so much an indication of his feelings as they were a reflection of attitudes of the 1930s which he believed he had to satisfy if he expected to get his manuscript published. Accordingly, such expressions as "a most horrible and sordid custom," "this barbarous ritual," and "this revolting custom" have been omitted. Other changes have included a few grammatical corrections and the placing of chapters in a more logical order than existed in the original document. The actual changes in the text, however, have been minimal. The wide and varied vocabulary, the writing style, and the factual details are all his.

This book is a joint venture of the Glenbow-Alberta Institute and the Blood Tribal Council and has been made possible through a grant from the Alberta Indian Treaties Commemoration Program, office of the Native Secretariat, government of Alberta.

HUGH A. DEMPSEY

Preface

THE FACTS RELATED in the following chapters concerning the lives of my people are presented from the viewpoint of an Indian. Often, in perusing supposedly authentic historic volumes, I have read of the Indians as being bloodthirsty individuals, yelling, whooping, and seeking to destroy. I have become increasingly aware, as I continued reading, that very few of the good points of the Indians were chronicled. Hence it became my desire to narrate as accurately as possible some of the true facts concerning my people, without exaggeration of their virtues or glossing over of their faults.

Doubtless, many people have wondered what were the feelings of the aborigines as they put aside their native garb and customs and began to take up life as civilized beings. In the following chapters I have tried to give as accurately and concisely as possible an account of my people's habits, customs, and mode of living, and, what is perhaps much less understood, some of the mental processes of my race. I also wish to acquaint the reader with a few "inside facts" which may help to establish a closer feeling of kinship between the white man and the red, and thus prevent either from experiencing that feeling of revulsion on meeting which cannot be better depicted than in the Indian expression 'Ugh!'

MIKE MOUNTAIN HORSE

CHAPTER ONE

The Blood Tribe

THE BLOOD INDIAN tribe, whose reserve lies north of Cardston in Alberta, comprises a component part in the great Blackfoot Indian Confederacy. In the year 1877 the federal administration of Canada decided to negotiate and conclude a treaty with these plains Indians of Western Canada. September 17th of that memorable year saw various western tribes under their respective chiefs, converging on Blackfoot Crossing to meet the Queen Mother's representatives in council.

The successful termination of this famous meeting after five days' deliberations by the numerous participants were due to the presence and influence on the Indians of Colonel James F. Macleod, who was one of the commissioners appointed to negotiate with the tribesmen. The ability of this officer, whose word was his bond, was held very highly in the estimation of the different chiefs.

As an example let me relate an incident how *Stamix-oto-kan*—Colonel Macleod's Indian name—was held by the natives under his jurisdiction. When the negotiations were in progress, Red Crow, head chief of the Blood tribe, arose to deliver his famous eloquent speech favoring acquiescence by his tribe to the stipulations of the treaty as interpreted to them.

His oratory endeavor is in part as follows: "I leave every-

Red Crow, head chief of the Blood tribe from 1870 to 1900.

thing to Stamix-oto-kan, because he never broke his word and kept all his promises to me. I trust him entirely. For that reason I agree to the terms offered to us by our Queen Mother."

This is worthy of note because stupendous is the task accomplished when an intruder—as the white man was considered then—can command the respect of the natives as Colonel Macleod did in the infancy of this great West.

Red Crow, lineal descendant of great ruling chieftains, was a tall quiet stately figure with piercing black eyes in a face which was beaming with intelligence. His quiet disposition did not radiate his warlike qualities, for he was rated as one of the greatest warriors of his day; his epics have been handed down to the present generation. The true Indian rhetoric and prodigality of languages were very noticeable in his numerous addresses to his people who loved and respected him for his two noble outstanding qualities: first as a native statesman in directing the affairs of his people, and lastly a great warrior, for to hear him relate his tales at the Sun Dances was enough to thrill the young warriors who were within hearing of his voice.

This was the man who was placing his people's future in the hands of *Stamix-oto-kan,* a white man. On Sept. 22nd, Red Crow applied his signature to the historic document to be followed by the other chiefs of his people.

The above treaty is officially known as Treaty No. Seven. Its signatories were the plains Indians of western Canada, represented by their leading chiefs such as the renowned Crowfoot, Red Crow, and many others. Second party to the agreement was the government of Canada. Here representatives were Honorable David Laird, lieutenant-governor of the North-West Territories, and the above mentioned Lt.-Col. Macleod, superintendent of the red coats, who made the hazardous march to the great unknown west a few years previous to the historic event.

Among the stipulations chronicled in this treaty was a clause that all Indian tribes whose chiefs were signatories would be allotted reserves where they were to reside. Possession of these reserves by my people were to be in perpetuity. Other minor clauses provided for a first payment of $12 per head and an annuity of $5 every year after for each Indian. Educational facilities for the Indian children were also to be the responsibility of the government of the day; boundaries were set for each respective reserve after they were allotted to each tribe.

Feeding of my people was not included in the clauses of the treaty because this expenditure was undertaken by the government on a verbal agreement with the chiefs. Another item stipulated $2,000 was to be appropriated by the government each year to provide firearms and ammunition for the tribesmen who wished to go hunting and to secure food. Another stipulation provided for hunting areas for the Indians on surrendered land. This clause is unequivocal in its meaning because it guaranteed unrestricted movement of hunting parties.

The Indian chief readily acquiesced to the treaty, but this was subject to regulations at intervals as may be passed by the government regarding settlement and the progress of civilization.

Numerous other minor articles were also embodied in the treaty. Under the agreement as decided upon, the Blood tribe was allotted their present reserve surrounded by the St. Mary's and the Belly Rivers, where they settled down to the prosiac pursuits and abandoned their nomadic fighting existence.

We Indians by slow degrees have tried hard to adjust ourselves to the new environment. After years of endeavor by the missionaries we are showing signs of civilization as inculcated to us in the schools provided for our education.

Here I must say the Mounted Police rendered invaluable assistance to the government during this period of transition of my people. I am sure without them and the influence of Colonel Macleod, the process of assimilating the habits and customs of the white race would have been much slower.

Coming upon the reserves which were allotted to them under the terms of the treaty, my people built numerous log huts along the river bottom of their reserve. Raising pony herds was their specialty. They also tilled some potato crops, but mostly were fed by the government. Twice a week rations of meat and flour were issued on these occasions. But mostly some of the Indians spent their time around adjacent towns, indulging in tea drinking contests and gambling to the extent of betting their clothes they were wearing. I remember Night Howler, a Blood Indian, getting home from a gambling expedition bereft of all his clothes excepting his moccasins and breechcloth.

To try and teach the Indian in his wild, primitive state was a stupendous undertaking by the missionaries who first went among these plains inhabitants. A missionary approaching an Indian village would cause a stampede by half-naked little savages for a nearby bush. The Indian department doctor would also cause a commotion in camp, because we Indian children held a mortal fear of vaccination, which generally was the cause of the doctor's visit to our camp. I have been a participant in these stampedes for a bush on numerous occasions along with other children of our camp. One instance stands out very clear in my mind although childish impressions are very vague.

Two little girls, about six and seven years of age, were among some children who were running into the shelter of a nearby bush on the special occasion. These little girls held their stone-blind aunt by each arm and were taking her along in their flight from the doctor to the bush, for fear the missionary who was approaching the camp would take her away to attend school and vaccinate her.

Eventually a day school on the Blood Reserve was started by the missionaries, and here was another problem. If one can picture the extreme difficulty of interesting, indifferent and even rebellious young natives in their studies to the extent of writing in English, perhaps they will grant these noble missionaries more praise for their Godly endeavor.

All of us children attending these day schools would show up with painted faces, wearing breech cloths and blankets, and teacher would give us one biscuit of hardtack to insure our attendance for the next day. At times some of the more timid ones would escape, the teacher after them, holding a biscuit as a lure to return. One would naturally come near enough to take the biscuit, when our teacher would seize the obstinate one and pull him into the schoolhouse.

We passed our time in drawing pictures on our slates, anything that suited our fancy to portray. Some drew a man in war paint dancing; others drew a warrior on horseback chasing buffalo. These were the problems our teachers had to contend with in their work among us in early days.

Residential schools were built on the Blood Reserve about the year 1889; both Roman Catholic and Protestant made the initial endeavor in the first real step forward towards educations for the Indian.

The Blood Indians have developed into a fine race of farmers. Fields of grain may be observed stretching for miles. The tentacles of civilization have engulfed the Indian. Our spectacular old timers are fast disappearing. In their place is a different race of Indians who have embraced the faith, also the habits and customs of the white race.

CHAPTER TWO

Childhood

MY OWN CHILDHOOD was like that of all Indian children. We spent our time playing, running and jumping. We ran about as wild and free as the birds, the young ones naked, and all of us scantily clad. Only when winter came did we don heavier clothing. One of my earliest recollections is a long caravan of Indians travelling to the nearest town to spend their annual treaty money. It was a cold winter day with snow over two feet deep on the ground. All the women were mounted on horseback with travois attached to the backs of their mounts.

A travois, it must be explained, is a device for carrying a child or baggage when going on a journey. Sometimes two small children are placed in one travois, but it is better for one alone.

Numerous children, I among them, were being carried on a travois on that particular day. It was rather uncomfortable at times to be sitting behind a horse with a long tail, especially when it took a notion to switch it right into your face.

Arriving at our destination the whole caravan repaired to a large flat near the river. Our men folk immediately went to the huge stove fire that served to heat a store, all ready to cater to us Indians. Here they loafed for a while and warmed themselves while our mothers, and other women folk, got to

A trading party of Bloods was photographed on the outskirts of Fort Macleod in the 1890s.

work. Using brush wood tied together as brooms, they swept away the snow from an area sufficiently large to put up their tepees. After these were erected, firewood was gathered by our mothers, who started the fires in our lodges so as to make them warm and cosy for us children. After a while the men returned from town laden with parcels, usually fat meat and white man's bread. Hard, long stick candy was portioned out to us children, which we gladly accepted, licking it as we played. We remained in town on this annual shopping expedition until all our money was spent, when we returned to our reserve.

I remember riding in a travois on another such shopping trip. When my people reached the town at dusk, they immediately went up to the stores while I was left sitting in the travois amid hundreds of horses tied to hitching posts. After a while my horse somehow got loose and started to walk away, grazing as it went along. Luckily for me it was quite gentle. This horse had gone a considerable distance when I disengaged myself from the travois and got out. It was quite dark by this time, and as I was only a baby I quickly lost all sense of direction. The last thing I remember I was trying to get back to where I thought the town lay. I was unconscious when they found me next morning, but I was a sturdy child and soon recovered.

I remember at night we gathered around the tepee fires of our homes, our eyes glistening in the firelight, and listened while some warrior related tales of valour or sang songs lauding our great men on the battle field. We boys, stirred by these tales, would leap into the circle and declare that we, too, would become mighty men, so that the tribe would honour us.

Thus the carefree days passed. Childish impressions are very vague and it is hard to define them, but I do remember that the feeling of Indian children who first came in contact with the white man was akin to terror, especially if he wore a beard or moustache. In their opinion he was supernatural, or, in other words a ghost. Let me give you a couple of instances, the first one concerning myself, which will show the fear an Indian child had for one who grew a beard or moustache.

It happened when I was a child. My brother, Hay Chief, and I were playing a hundred yards or so from our parents' tepee when I heard mother calling, "Look out! See who's coming!" I looked around and saw a white man with a beard coming toward us. Like a streak of lightning I made for home, yelling and crying for my mother.

On another occasion many generations ago, a large encampment of Indians were aroused from slumber one morning by a young Indian riding into camp on a spirited horse. This boy had ridden hard to inform the camp that a strange being was walking towards them. "There is a creature heading in this direction," he said. "He has hair all over his face, wears long hair, and has two legs like a human being. He appears as if he came out of a hole in the ground."

The camp at once broke into turmoil, women diving into the nearby brush with screaming babies hanging on to their buckskin shirts, warriors mounted on chargers chanting battle songs. Some of the more intrepid men rode out to meet this terrible creature. The stranger stood still at sight of the approaching riders, grinding the knuckles of his right hand on his right jaw, a sign among the Indians indicating the Peigan tribe. The astonished warriors rode up and greeted him. He turned out to be an old prospector who had been travelling with the Blackfoot in Montana; hence his knowledge of the sign language.

"Look out! Don't cry any more. There's Standing Alone

coming this way. He'll throw you in the river if you don't behave!"

That warning came from my mother one cold winter morning, in our tepee home on the Blood Reserve. I was in a very fractious mood, venting my childish feelings at intervals in loud, lustrous yells, accompanied by copious tears. The reason for my unseemly conduct was dislike for having my hair combed and braided, a common enough objection among Indian children.

It may be surprising to learn that the first native inhabitants made a practice each morning of throwing their children into ice-covered creeks and rivers—whichever was available. Their reason for doing so was to harden the child's constitution against adverse weather conditions, thus fortifying him against sickness.

I can well remember being subjected to this peculiar practice as a child. One morning I was curled up warm in bed when I was rudely awakened by Bacon, an Indian of our camp, who pulled the blankets off and seized me under one arm. I kicked, screamed, and fought, but in spite of that, Bacon carried me to the river and waded in up to his waist. He then ordered me to dive. I dipped my nose under the water like a duck.

"No!" he yelled, "Do like this," accompanying his words by diving.

When he came up I was still standing. My tormentor started to splash me so vigorously that I did a submarine act and dived. My brown, naked little body turned pink from the effects of my sudden submersion and I ran home as fast as possible, Bacon following me, grunting like a hog to speed me on. Father paid a blanket to Bacon for thus assisting me in my ablutions.

Sometimes when there was a layer of ice on the river, a hole sufficiently large to enable the child to have his swim was kicked into it. Every male Indian child received this elementary training in order to fit him for the career of hunter and fighter.

Another custom imposed on the Indian child was that of piercing the lobes of the ears so as to have them ready for earrings. The piercing was done by an old Indian woman with a sharp bone when the child was very young and his ears still tender.

On rare occasions an Indian child of teen age was punished. In winter time a naughty youth was taken out, stripped naked, and rolled around in deep snow, and the snow kicked in his face.

The training of Indian youth in warfare was a very simple matter. Every male child, when able to ride, was given a pony by his parents. On some occasions during the summer months hundreds of boys, under the leadership of older lads, assembled on their ponies at a point about a mile or so from the main tribal encampment. Here they proceeded to daub themselves from head to foot with clay, leaves and brush found along the river beds, using some of the latter as head gear. These mounted figures then rode slowly in the direction of their main camp, chanting in unison the war songs of their elders. Natural cover was taken advantage of by these lads in order to approach their objective unobserved. At the most opportune time, amid yells and war whoops, they charged at a gallop on the unsuspecting camp.

The object of these raids was to grab as much buffalo meat as possible from the camp. This meat was hung out on tripods to dry, and it was up to the women on these occasions to defend it. Long strips of the meat were used as weapons to beat off the clay-covered invaders. During the melee some of the raiders came off victorious while others who ran into stout opposition retired without the coveted prize. Converging again at the starting point, the raiders enjoyed their buffalo meat which they cooked over hot wood ashes, placing some of the choice tidbits before their leaders who, like the "arm-chair" warriors, had remained in camp. These innocuous raids were staged at intervals during the summer time and thus the Indian youth of the plains received his intial training in warfare.

The natural weapon of war used by the Indian, we all know, was the bow and arrow. So quite naturally every boy was an expert bowman. He was capable of splitting with his arrow a small wand placed upright in the ground at approximately 25 yards distance.

Adults made bows and arrows for their children. When a young lad was able to handle them he joined the archery competitions which were held each evening among the boys. One of these contests consisted of teams shooting at small sticks about a quarter inch in diameter placed vertically in the ground at a distance of ten to 25 yards. After all the contestants had shown their skill, amid loud singing and shouting, the nearest arrows to the target of each team were measured. If identical in distance, each winning competitor must repeat his shot, but not at the stick. A small bundle of brush tied together, about four inches in length and two inches in diameter, was thrown up in the air, and whoever pierced the moving target first was adjudged the winner in the contest. This gave his team the privilege of collecting any arrows shot by their opponents which were left on the ground.

Another great pastime enjoyed by Indian youth was hawk-hunting with bows and arrows. Taking advantage of any cover, the Indian lad crept up on his intended victim perched high and majestic on the top of a tree and brought it down with one sure swift shot. The wings and tail feathers were then plucked, the wings to be used as fans for the older members of the tribe, and the tail feathers for making arrows.

Gopher hunting was another favorite sport of these stalwart sons of the plains. To prove his skill, the boy had to hit the little animal while it was running.

To make a bow and arrow, a man took a number of small willow sticks about a quarter inch in diameter and cut them into lengths of about three feet. He peeled the bark off clean and lay them out in the sun to dry. Then he took some of the flight feathers of a hawk and cut them about three inches long. He split each feather in two and held one end with his teeth and the other end taught, running his knife to and fro on the scabrous edge of the quills to make them pliable and easy to adjust. He prepared three halves in this manner. Then he took some sinew which had previously been thoroughly soaked and pulled out a strand of it, twisting it once around the thick end of a prepared stick. One of the half feathers was trimmed about one-eighth of an inch at the top, leaving that portion of the quill bare, and the sinew already on the stick was wound over the bare end of the first quill. He repeated this procedure with the second feather and finally with the third, winding the sinew neatly. He did not tie a knot but just pressed it on when it dried as it would shrink securely in place.

He followed the same method with the sinew at the lower end of the three feathers. When the task was accomplished, he trimmed all three feathers alike for guiding purposes. Next, he cut a V-shaped groove at the feathered end of the stick for the bow string and split the other end. There he inserted his arrow head and tied the split stick together with sinew. Now he had a finished arrow.

For the bow, he cut a piece of saskatoon wood about four feet long and trimmed it flat at both ends, leaving about six inches in the middle for gripping purposes. Notches were cut about an inch from each of the two ends and the bow string of sinew cord tied at one of the notches. He then bent the bow to the required angle and tied the other end. Now the bow and arrow were ready for any emergency.

Bows used in warfare and for hunting the buffalo were slightly different. Both were nearly straight which required considerable strength to bend them, thereby sending the arrows on their way with terrific force and considerable speed. Indian archers were known to send an arrow right through the thick hide of a buffalo.

Another game played by young Bloods was a battle of stone tops. This game was played on ice between two boys. Egg or cone-shaped rocks served as tops. The bark of a white bush similar to the snowdrop, and common on our river bottoms, was first peeled off and the yellow inside coating taken out. The latter comes out in long strands, four to five feet long. This was braided and a whip made out of it. After adjusting a two-foot handle, the two rivals spun their tops and whipped them until they hummed. These were then made to collide with considerable force and the top which remained spinning the longest was declared the winner. As a boy I often played others far into the starry night clashing tops, and we derived much innocent fun out of this game.

Still another popular contest between two Indian boys was called "shooting sticks." The sticks used were the same size and a little longer than an arrow. The bark was peeled off and the stick left out in the sun to dry. After drying, the teeth were used in straightening them out. In playing this game as many sticks as desired could be used, but both sides had to have the same number. A small depression in the ground, with a little slant, was selected. Each contestant gripped the base of a stick in his right hand, placing the tip of his fourth finger on the end. He then threw his stick with a backward, downward and forward curve motion of the arm on the slant ground. I have witnessed contestants shooting sticks 100 yards in this way. After each boy had shot all his sticks, the contestant shooting the farthest would gather up the sticks of his opponent as his prize.

Sleighing in winter time was another amusement the Indian boy enjoyed. Buffalo ribs were tied together with rawhide thongs in rows about three feet wide and were used as sleighs. Buffalo tails were attached to the rear for decorative purposes. Toboggan rides were taken on these unique sleighs made of buffalo ribs and they provided much merriment and fun.

The Indian child made his own toys. He showed great aptitude in moulding such animals as horses, buffalo and birds of all kinds. After these clay toys had been dried in the sun they would last a long time. They were never taken into the tepees, but were left out on the banks where the clay was most available, and if they were destroyed in a storm, the children set to work to make new ones.

The most primitive sport was a mud battle fought by young tribesmen. Sides were picked, and the two bands of Indian boys would repair to a large flat under their respective leaders, each boy armed with a long pliable switch about six feet long and a big ball of mud weighing about 20 pounds. Here the opposing leaders would take up their positions, a distance of about 75 yards separating them. Each fighter would then take a small piece of mud weighing about four ounces and press it hard on the tip of his switch. The flexibility of a switch would send these mud pellets flying with terrific force and they would burn and leave bruises on the body of anyone unfortunate enough to be struck by them. A battle of this kind would rage sometimes for hours, mud whistling through the air accompanied by loud yells from those in the casualty list. After the cessation of hostilities everyone was happy, despite the sore spots and numerous bruises discernable on the bodies of the combatants.

Do we wonder now that the Indian was a born warrior? From his childhood fighting was inculcated into his young mind. Naturally he aspired to that position in his tribe which would bring him honor as a great and noble warrior.

CHAPTER THREE

Early Years

M Y PEOPLE, THE Blood Indians, are banded together with three other tribes as part of the Blackfoot Confederacy. At Treaty No. Seven in 1877, each tribe was allotted a piece of land on which to live, and all have kept in close contact with one another.

The Blood Indians first lived in log huts along the river bottom of their reserve. One of their chief industries was raising pony horses; another was the tilling of potato crops, when the spirit moved them. Earlier, they had spent most of their time being debauched in nearby forts, trading beautiful buffalo robes for a few gallons of diluted whiskey. The white trader would mix one gallon of whiskey and four gallons of water, and trade this mixture to an Indian for about 40 buffalo hides, valued at ten dollars each, the tanning of which represented the winter's work of the women.

Owing to the nomadic habits of the Blood Indians, any attempt of the early missionaries to teach them was a stupendous undertaking. I can still envision the approach of a missionary to an Indian village. A stampede of half naked little children for the nearby brush would be the first intimation of his approach.

After we settled on reserves, these missionaries visited our

Indian camps periodically to enroll pupils for the day schools opened by some of the churches. Bull Shield's day school on the Blood Reserve (Chief Bull Shields, for whom this school was named, was my uncle) was the first school I attended, but I do not remember any book learning acquired there. A bell was rung each morning to announce that school was opened. We all usually showed up with painted faces, breech clouts, and a blanket. To insure his attendance the next day, each child was given a biscuit of hardtack before leaving. Some of the more timid pupils would occasionally escape through the back door when teacher's back was turned.

My people, fed as destitutes by the government at that time, had no particular desire to work and settle down, but travelled from one reserve to another, indulging in tea drinking contests. These contests were carried on according to certain rules, clan against clan. It was a common occurrence for the assembled contestants to drink about fifty gallons of tea a night. Each side brought their own pails and tea, brewing the beverage to the quantity desired. Thus it went on all night.

In 1893, when I was six years old, I was sent to St. Paul's Residential School. The need for such an institution had been recognized by the missionary societies in eastern Canada, and a boys' home had been erected on the Blood Reserve. The building of this school in 1889, by Rev. Mr. Sam Trivett who taught there until 1891, was the beginning of a new period of advancement for the Indians. When the boys' home was opened in 1893, the leading Indian chiefs who had asked the Indian Commissioner for such a home, set a good example by enrolling their own boys first. The enrolment of pupils at this school came in the following order: John Day Chief, Willie Scraping White, Charlie Good Rider, Tom Spear Chief, Fred Mountain Horse, Ben Strangling Wolf, and Mike Mountain Horse. I was therefore one of the first pupils to be enrolled at St. Paul's.

My father brought me to the school one cold winter morning. After the entry of my name in the school books by Harry Swainson, the boys' overseer, my brother Fred, then a pupil at the school, took me in charge. My Indian clothes, consisting of blanket, breech cloth, leggings, shirt and moccasins, were removed. Then my brother took me into another room where I was placed in a steaming brown fibre paper tub full of water. Yelling blue murder, I started to jump out, but my brother held on to me and I was well scrubbed and placed before a heater to dry. Next came Mr. Swainson with a pair of shears. I was again placed in a chair. Zip went one of my long braids to the floor: the same with the other side. A trim was given as a finish to my haircut. My brother again took me in charge. "Don't cry any more," he said. "You are going to get nice clothes." Mrs. Swainson then came into the room with a bundle of clothes for me: knee pants, blouse to match with a wide lace collar, a wee cap with an emblem sewn in front, and shoes. Thus attired I strutted about like a young peacock before the other pupils.

The general enclosure of the school was in the form of a fenced oblong, at the south end of which were three buildings: the girls' home at one corner, a store room in the centre, and at the other corner, the stable. On the west side were two buildings, one of which served as our church and school room, and the other the boys' home. The north end of the enclosure at that time had only the gate to grace its boundary. Later, a principal's house was erected there. The east side of the oblong contained two further buildings—the hospital and another store room. This entire little educational centre was situated just off the Blood Reserve on a large island which was bounded on one side by the Belly River and on the other by a creek which returned, after partly encircling the island, to the river. Strangely enough, the Indians never accepted St. Paul's as the proper name of the school colony, but always referred to it as "Big Island." So firmly did they adhere to that appellation that the school which was subsequently moved to the Cardston area was still "Big Island" to the tribe.

At the time of my arrival at the school the principal was the Rev. Frank Swainson, from whose name the Indians adapted one more typical of their own style. He was called by them, in their own language, "Swan." His brother, the overseer, was dubbed a more personal title for apparently other reasons, being spoken of as "Handsome."

Some of the pupils, myself included, had the great pleasure of meeting "Swan" in London, during the Great War. We had a great and lasting affection for Mr. Swainson, and it is doubtful if he deserved the criticisms which he afterwards received for seeming extravagances. His vast generosity undoubtedly depleted his grocery and other stores. But who shall say that he did not thereby gain the co-operation of parents which otherwise could not have been procured? Then there were the wonderful Christmas presents which he lavished on us. But who can deny that this was a most forceful and practical way of making us realize the true import of that greatest of Christian festivals? Lastly (and this was a real waste?) his

Rev. and Mrs. Frank Swainson (back) worked with students on the nearby Peigan Reserve before becoming missionaries among the Bloods.

granting to us of gifts, provided we solicited the same in a note written in English. If the reader can picture the extreme difficulty of interesting indifferent and even at times rebellious young natives in their studies, to the extent of writing an English note, he will perhaps have more sympathy for the good "Swan" than had many of his critics.

When the writer was six or seven years old, he became aware that if a note written in English, containing a request for some gift, was laid on the Reverend Swainson's desk, there was a great possibility that the request would be granted. Now an Indian boy, even though well fed at the school, had a psychological reaction to "valuable gifts." Indeed, his range of known desirables was somewhat limited. So my first note contained a very laboured request for a pound of butter and one can of milk, and when I went to claim them, they were both given to me. Alas! I had no use for either and they were thrown away.

But one is forced to admit that without this little gift game there was the possibility that no further interest in writing English notes would have been experienced by the writer. Thus the so-called extravagances of Mr. Swan may have been economies insofar as educational results among the Indian pupils were concerned.

In addition to being our principal, Mr. Swainson was also our preacher. Contrary to school procedure the church services were conducted in the Blackfoot tongue so that we might more easily assimilate the teachings relative to the great God of the white man who had created all things and ruled over all. And here again, Mr. Swainson showed his forcefulness among the Indians, for with faith created by our confidence in him, we accepted without question the new Diety. While this was done without the proverbial grain of salt, it must be confessed that the powerful sway of the new was not sufficient to entirely dethrone the many spirits to whom we had previously made our offerings, and that state of affairs has been maintained to the present day.

Owing to ill health, Mr. Swainson resigned in 1895, and several changes in principals were made thereafter until the Rev. S. H. Middleton was appointed in the year 1910.

CHAPTER FOUR

Christmas Day

$\mathbf{M}$Y EARLIEST RECOLLECTION of Santa Claus and his reindeer was in the year 1894, my first Christmas in school at St. Paul's Mission. In those early days Christmas services were held in log huts on our reserves. Any available hut was utilized by these early missionaries for this purpose. Their congregations consisted mostly of men who squatted on their varied colored blankets on the earthen floor. A few women also attended. We children, almost naked, would make ourselves a nuisance by continually running back and forth to the hut where the service was being held. Scores of skinny, mangey mongrels of all descriptions would also converge at the place of worship. Frequently these latter would start a fight among themselves causing a great deal of excitement among the children who would try to separate their pets from the other combatants. Our parents' main reason for bringing their children to hear the "Holy White Man," as they called him, was the supply of hard candy which was distributed to us at the close of the service. He would also invite our parents to his little home and hand out clothes such as coats, scarves, mitts, and various other useful items, as Christmas presents. This was in the 1890s.

About the only Indian of our tribe who celebrated Yuletide

in his home at that time was Joe Healy. He also had an "at home" for the Indians in general. Everybody was welcome at these gatherings. Great preparations were made for this special day when Flying Chief—as he was called—was going to feed his friends. From early morning to late at night wagons loaded with Indians, men, women and children, would be seen driving from all parts of the reserve toward Healy's house, numerous dogs following in their wake. A few men rode horseback, while an occasional woman might be observed, with her papoose sitting contentedly in a travois which her mount was carrying. Any Indians whose cabins were in close proximity to Joe's house arrived on foot to enjoy the hospitality of Mr. Healy and his good wife. A long table laden with juicy roasts, vegetables of all kinds, and numerous cakes, awaited them, and everybody sat down to do full justice to the feast. A little bag filled with apples, candy and peanuts was handed to each child at the conclusion of this feast. The women were also given parcels of food for those of their families who were unable to attend.

Now let me relate an amusing incident that occurred to

One of the prominent families on the Blood Reserve was that of Joe Healy, seen here with his family. Left to right are Topitkinee (Mrs. Healy), Wolf Moccasin (Mr. Healy), Joe, Jr. (on lap), John, David (in front) and Amy.

Mr. Healy in his endeavor to make a very happy Christmas
for his children. At that time Mr. Healy had three children who
had not yet been enrolled at the residential school and were
still home with him. These were Johnny, Mary and Janie.
Christmas Eve arrived. Mrs. Healy cautioned her offspring
to behave and go to sleep early because Old Man—the Indian
name for Santa Claus—was coming that night to give each one
of them a present. But these children, curious to see Santa
Claus, and a little fearful of what he might do to them if they
were asleep when he arrived, stayed awake. Johnny occupied
the edge of their bed, taking this position as protector of his two
younger sisters who occupied the space nearest the wall.

Along towards morning Santa Claus came in cautiously
with a bag on his back. Johnny, ever on the alert, espied him
first, and thinking him to be a ghost of some description, or
someone coming to do them harm, jumped out of bed and,
seizing the broom, started to inflict a very telling barrage of
blows on Santa Claus. This unexpected reception caused him
to retire in quick order, yelling as he did so, "Son, you are
hurting me!" Thus did Santa Claus let the cat out of the bag!

As time passed a large number of children were enrolled
at the different schools erected on our reserve. Great excitement
prevailed at the schools as the "Big Holy Day" approached.
I remember distinctly my first contact with Santa Claus during
my first year at school. I was only five at the time. We children
had paraded to our school room where a large Christmas tree
stood laden with gifts for all. After a short wait there was a
great commotion near the entrance. Jingle bells could be heard
outside and some of the staff laughingly ran towards the door
to ascertain the cause of the uproar. An old man with a huge
stomach and a white beard then made his appearance. Some
of us children began to scream loudly and crawl under every
available school desk. Others got behind some of the teachers,
holding on to their legs for dear life. One boy named Arthur
White Buffalo did the ostrich stint by sticking his head into a
big cast-iron heater. It was some time before our teachers could
calm us and not before we saw Santa Claus drop down on the
floor, scattering a huge bag of candy, apples and peanuts in
all directions, which caused his stomach to diminish in size.
After this we enjoyed Santa Claus's visit, especially when he
began to distribute the numerous gifts from the Christmas tree.

After that first year I always looked forward with great joy
to Christmas Day. As time passed the Spirit of Goodwill spread
among us Indians generally. Different lodges undertook the

task of playing host to others at big dances and feasts. Unlike the white people, who solicit public donations for any charitable enterprise, the Indian societies require their members to contribute towards any undertaking sponsored in their name.

I remember one Christmas "at home" sponsored by the secret Horn Society. Each of its officers donated ten dollars and five dollars was contributed by the rank and file. The sum thus collected enabled this society to entertain at a great feast and dance not only local Indians but also visiting tribesmen from other reserves. At these Christmas dances visiting Indians were given a place of honor at the back of the hall facing the entrance. A visiting Indian was not required to dance unless asked to do so by a local woman, who gives him a present for this privilege. In all Indian dances the ladies ask the men to dance with them.

Now let us imagine ourselves participating at a Christmas dance and feast on the Blood Reserve. A large hall, built with round walls, serves as a community hall. Here all Christmas dances are held. The society officiating as host at a Christmas dance and feast assigns various duties to its members. One will be required to haul firewood and water to the community hall. Others will be detailed to clean out and decorate. One member will be asked to arrange for lights and coal oil, and a young man will be detailed to chop up all wood available for heating purposes.

People start arriving at the hall at about dusk. Wagon loads of Indians coming over the hills will be seen at intervals. A young man riding his pony will be seen approaching the hall, singing at the top of his voice. Hundreds of Indians in festive mood congregate to celebrate this greatest of all Christian festivals. Strange faces will be noticed among those present. These are visitors from neighboring reserves. They are quickly led forward by one of the committee and given seats on the floor in the space reserved for visitors. Seating arrangements are cared for by placing all women on one side and men on the opposite. A platform in the centre is reserved for drummers and singers. Boxes of groceries are also piled high in the centre.

Dancing begins to the beating of drums and singing. This is kept up at intermittent intervals, the braves dancing by themselves first, followed by the ladies asking the men to dance with them. Lunch is served at midnight, three or four chieftains playing hosts on this occasion, and a corresponding number of table cloths spread out on the floor. The guests sit around these table cloths. A progressive Indian playing host would have his wife bake cakes, pies and loaf bread for this special occasion. A less progressive host would have boiled meat and fried bread on his table cloth.

I remember a Christmas party which I attended on the Peigan Reserve. One of the hosts at a table cloth spread on the floor was an old Indian named Big Face Chief. I had noticed the old fellow after he started to spread his cloth. First he got hold of a huge pan of buns which he scattered broadcast all over the cloth. Then someone called to him from the opposite side of the hall. He immediately kicked the buns aside with his toes and walked across the table cloth. Later, I heard my name called as a guest at this particular table cloth. My excuse of having "just had supper" was ignored by a huge brave who led me forward by my right arm to the array of buns, and I sat down with a number of other Indians. I managed to slip a few of the buns in my pocket when no one was looking, which I later distributed to a gathering of boys loitering outside.

At these Christmas parties and dances the boxes of groceries piled high in the centre of the hall were given out as presents to aged people and visitors. Many hundred pounds of sugar were given out; jams of all descriptions, meat and bread were also issued. Candies, apples, and peanuts were not forgotten. Presents also were given to visiting Indians. These were in the form of money, bedding and clothing. The dance concluded about daylight, when all retire to their respective homes, sleepy and tired after the night's festivities.

Different schools on the reserve also celebrated an Indian day for Christmas. These took the form of huge feasts consisting of plum pudding and various other good things. An Indian school was a beehive of activity on such a day. Long hours of labor by the school staff were required to make a success of this undertaking. There is a saying that "an Indian treats his stomach as his god." Well, we sure did full justice to the hospitality of the school staff on such days and looked forward to the next time when we should again be invited. Hundreds of Indians from all parts of the reserve gathered on these occasions and everyone was treated to a good dinner. After everyone had adjourned to the school house, Santa Claus visited this huge gathering of tribesmen, where he distributed presents such as useful bits of clothing, overcoats, scarves and mitts.

As the season of Christmas drew near, towns and cities were visited by Indians in up-to-date cars, for the purpose of doing their Christmas shopping. Numerous toys were sold to the visiting tribesmen and many a little Indian child's wish was granted by good Santa Claus on Christmas morning.

Family parties were the order of the day at Christmas time, when Indians had the privilege of having with them their children, who were attending residential schools. Huge roasted turkey, with all the trimmings, was the chief item on an Indian Christmas menu. High-class concerts were given by the pupils of the various Indian schools. The entertainments these Indian children participated in would do credit to them if staged in any big city.

CHAPTER FIVE

A Warrior's Life

THE BLOOD INDIANS were always noted as a fierce and powerful tribe. They spent most of their time travelling over the western country, hunting, fighting their foes, and at times enjoying to the utmost their quiet life in beautiful places where bountiful supplies of wood and water were available.

Their home life began in a tepee and they loved this home. The original buffalo skin tepees had been discarded prior to my boyhood days, but the later canvas type were more portable, easier to erect, and I have a very happy recollection of the one which constituted my home.

In the centre of the tepee was a hearth where a large fire kept the lodge cosy and warm, regardless of what the spirits were sending in the way of cold weather. All around the sides of the tepee walls beds were made up, and at the back of each bed, from the poles of the tepee, was hung a tanned hide on which was painted a fancy design. These designs were to the Indians what pictures on the walls are to the white man.

Our paints in those days consisted of baked earth colored with the juices of berries. The paint pots were made from buffalo horns cut to the shape of small bowls. The brushes used by the artists who, by the way, were usually women, were made of small bones and the "bristles" were the ragged edges of the same bone. For sewing purposes sinew from the buffalo were utilized in lieu of thread.

Among the Bloods, a woman, past the age of early youth, became a drudge. She gathered the supply of firewood at all times. When a move was ordered, she dismantled the tepee and erected it again at the new place chosen by her husband. She attended to the dressing of the skins, the making of clothes and the preparation of food, as well as sundry other even more menial tasks. While travelling, the Indian woman assumed the heavy burden of the labor for, apart from the making of war weapons and pipes, the men at home were veritable "gentlemen of leisure." In the summer and autumn they were busy waging war with their enemies and hunting buffalo, but with the beginning of the new year came the season of festivals, when the warriors had ceased their conflicts for the season, and even the women enjoyed a little leisure.

Gambling was a passion with most Indians. One game of chance after another claimed their attention during these slack months. That the betting was somewhat high, and that the participants were no pikers is proved by a story which was told to me by an old Indian named Three Guns. He said that once in mid-winter, with the snow three feet deep, the men of his village returned some distance from a gambling visit bereft of their leggings and barefoot, yet in excellent humor. I have often wondered, since hearing this tale, whether the white man knew anything of "strip poker" prior to his acquaintance with the Indians.

Interesting too was the procedure of an Indian feast. The invitations were extremely simple and informal, the host merely bidding his prospective guests, in a loud and sonorous voice, to come and eat. The invitation was always accepted, the guests bringing with them their own dishes and spoons— the latter a piece of shell. On arrival the visitors arranged themselves around the interior of the tepee, some squatting on the ground, others seating themselves on the beds along the walls. At a signal from the host, attending women filled the bowls and the feast commenced. That a good appetite was quite an ordinary thing in those days is to be inferred from the fact that feasting was often prolonged throughout the whole day.

The Indians had no written law. It is surprising therefore that people who were so fierce in their dealings with outsiders should have lived so peaceably together in large numbers. The explanation is that they were strongly influenced by customs and had a complete system of usages which controlled their inclinations and actions. They were always ready to help one another. When a young woman was married, her relatives supplied her with home commodities in order to give her a start in housekeeping. The people were, moreover, hospitable and sociable. The poor and outcast had only to enter a tepee and food was set before them. In addition to the dances and feasts, the Bloods indulged in considerable visiting among themselves, their talk on these occasions being chiefly of the prowess exhibited by them in recent battles.

All Indians were very superstitious and possessed their own ideas regarding nature. They believed that birds, beasts and reptiles could feel, perceive and reason as might a man, and that they possessed these qualities even after death. They also believed that they could hear human prayer and influence human life. Hence it is that an Indian has been known to make a long speech of apology to a bear that he had wounded, and to treat with great care and attention a bone of the dead for fear of offending its original owner. They believed, too, that in lakes, rivers and waterfalls dwelt spirits or living beings, and they strove to win the favour of these by means of gifts. For instance, whenever the Indians passed the Medicine Rock at Lethbridge, they cast a gift, usually tobacco, on the top and beside it, at the same time offering a prayer to the local spirit.

Dreams played an important part in the life on an Indian. They told him the cures for his infrequent ailments, taught him the position and place of his enemy, or the haunts of plentiful game for his hunting trip. He believed that the enactment of any natural phenomenon had potential effect for good or evil on his career, and not being always sure as to which result to expect, he was in constant fear. The fall of a leaf, the movement of an animal, or the cry of a bird, were to him tokens of either success and happiness, or failure and despair.

The Indian idea of a supreme being was somewhat vague. He had one word to express his conception of God, the literal translation of which is "He made us," and the appellation was not confined to any one deity but applied to any being or thing which was imagined to have more than human power. Such was the religious belief of the people who the pioneer missionaries found on the plains of the northwest of our continent.

In his dealings with the white intruders the Indian displayed two very marked characteristics—a love of freedom and a spirit of revenge. This untamed wanderer of the plains could only slowly submit to the restraints of a European civilization;

as the newcomers pushed inland from the Atlantic and central territories, he withdrew further west rather than part with his freedom. In his dealings with the Indian the settler was not always just, and his injustices drew down on him the vengeful enmity of a foe that never forgot an injury. Thus we find the early pages of Canadian history filled with the records of Indian warfare in all its horrors, the most hideous of which was the use of the scalping knife. This custom of removing the skin and top hair from a victim's head, native historians tell us originated as follows:

A great chief once offered his beautiful daughter in marriage to the brave who would fight and kill a certain member of a neighboring tribe. As proof of his deed he was to bring back the dead body of his victim. The young warrior who eventually succeeded in killing the enemy hastened home with the body to gain the coveted prize. Finding himself hotly pursued and his burden growing heavier, he was forced to cut it down bit by bit as he proceeded, in order to keep in advance of the avenging pursuers. Hence, when he reached home, nothing remained of his gruesome burden but the scalp. However, the chief deemed this sufficient evidence of his accomplishment and the warrior was given his daughter in marriage.

Although this story may be pure legend, there is no doubt that scalping was a general practice in Indian warfare, and for many years struck terror to the hearts of the early immigrants to this continent. From the white man's point of view it was a dastardly and cruel finish to an extremely primitive fight. But by the red man it was accepted as a spoil of war to which the victor was fully entitled, a penalty which he expected to undergo himself in case of defeat.

Authentic details of the life of the Indian and his household are seldom recounted, and almost never in full. So let us delve into the circumstances surrounding the early manhood of the Indian. Let us see if we can discover the origin of the war whoop, the design of each warrior's face painting, and the patterns portrayed on the tepee. In writing on these subjects I realize that human memory is liable to lapses but I have little fear of contradiction, since the information I have acquired comes directly from my father, a noted warrior who played an important role in numerous raids, with almost incredible daring, against hereditary foes of the Blackfoot Confederacy.

Suppose you imagine that you were in a battle with Blood warriors, you would doubtless interpret the hideous screeching of the encircling redskins as manifestations of bloodmadness in which each warrior tries to outdo his comrades. If you listen more carefully, however, you will notice that no two of the warriors are chanting or yelling similar war whoops but that each is carrying on an individual chant of his own. This naturally could only be understood if the listener were familiar with the dialect. On closer scrutiny it will also be observed that no two of the attackers have the same designs painted on their faces. Yet should you be able to identify any particular one, and could observe him at a future raid, you would find that the personal design of his war paint never varied.

Let us enquire therefore into the reasons for these individual "whoops" and "faces." Perhaps one of the best methods is to take a little excursion with one of the young men and study his entry into the ranks of the warriors. This was really the youthful Indian's qualification for attaining his maturity and all the qualities associated with a male adult.

As soon, then, as the young man was of mature age and was able to ride a horse and to handle proficiently the weapons of war, he had to be ready to attach himself to a party going on the warpath against the adversaries of his tribe. Indeed, in some cases, through clandestine trysts with confidants of another friendly tribe, he took up warfare on behalf of those other than his own people, for the Indian was a born fighter and took pride in no occupation so much as in warfare.

First he was presented by his father to some aged and renowned warrior of the tribe in whose interests he proposed to offer his services. After a preliminary ceremony with the parent, which involved a fairly heavy remuneration for his services, the old warrior blessed the youth and prayed for prosperity in his undertakings. He prayed that the boy would bring back a few head of horses and at least one captured rifle, the last being considered a signal honour. The prayers ended, the old man then proceeded to paint a certain design on the boy's face. This design the novice was compelled to memorize and to paint it—and no other—on his face prior to going into any hostile action. That is why each warrior's face was always painted in exactly the same style, no two being alike.

The next lesson imparted to the youth by the ancient warrior was the teaching of an original war chant which must be sung during the heat of conflict. This too had to be committed to memory and used by none other than he who received it as part of his training. And herein lies the secret of the terms "hideous," "unearthly," etc., applied by those who do not understand the origin of the war whoops or war chants. It would surprise me greatly if, supposing a large party of Indians had met a group of musical whites, each one singing a different popular air with the enthusiasm exhibited by the Indian on the warpath, the red men had not been put to utter flight. However, the gutterals of my native tongue may have had the effect of making the Indian chants more ferocious-sounding than can be imagined by one conversant with the dialect.

The following incident, which occurred during my service with the Canadian Expeditionary Force in France during World War One, is an amusing illustration of this point. One morning Jerry had been strafing us most unpleasantly. My discomfort was intense and finally, my nerves getting the better of me, I released my pent-up feelings in the rendering of my own particular war song. The first and most vociferous response came from an adjoining section of hefty Jocks who, wishing me to repeat this demonstration for the benefit of their officers, encored me vigorously. I declined to do so, however, and though some of my companions assured me that my war whoops had stopped the war for at least a few seconds, I have never been able to ascertain exactly what was Jerry's reaction to my outburst.

As a further step in the novice warrior's initiation, the instructor presented the youngster with a good luck mascot—perhaps bird feathers, rabbit's ears—anything he may have carried into battle during bygone days. This mascot the boy tied on top of his head and thus equipped prepared for his journey. His relatives supplied several pairs of moccasins and his weapons of war, and added to these was always a rope. Food was never carried for this had to be "rustled" en route. Whenever a stop was made, men were sent out to get meat from the nearest herd of buffalo, while others were appointed to erect a shelter for the night. When the provisioners returned and the party had feasted, a portion of the meat was cut into strips, hung to dry in the sun, and kept as a cache for use on the return journey. Any surplus of the remaining meat was cooked and carried. This procedure was adopted at any time that the food supply was low, thus assuring not only sustenance during the outward journey, but a supply on hand during the return journey, when time as well as food were likely to be very valuable.

As soon as the party reached hostile territory an advance scout was sent forward to reconnoitre the country ahead. This man pantomined from a distance the results of his observations, then pointed out the most suitable and strategic position for an attack by running back and forth on some prominent place from where he could be seen by his party. The main party then quietly advanced to the site selected. If the scout had merely discovered a lone wayfarer, the party immediately surrounded, captured and dispatched the unfortunate victim; a wild scramble for his scalp and rifle—the two most highly prized trophies of war—ensued. If a main camp of the enemy had been discovered, night was chosen as the most propitious time in which to approach and make the attack or, more usually, to steal any horses that were used as hunters; these usually were picketed among the tepees. Some warriors, more cautious than others, drove picket stakes inside their tepees, but the crafty invaders were equal to even this precaution, and went quietly to the horse, cut the rope near his head, and led him away while his unsuspecting master slept. When a satisfactory supply of horses had been secured the return journey commenced immediately in order to forestall discovery of the raid by the victims. Usually pursuit followed in a very few hours, the direction of the invaders being picked up by the trackers. This sometimes led to the nearest hilly and bushy country, where the invading tribe took up its position and made ready to fight for its illicit acquisitions. If their lucky star was shining, the flight was successfully continued; if not, a pitched battle followed and to the star's absence was attributed any defeat which may have ensued.

In these fierce battles many of the combatants fell, while others of the losing forces escaped. Those who were unfortunate enough to be captured were scalped, stripped and burned by their conquerors. The Indian was very cruel to his prisoners and the custom of scalping was calculated to give the maximum amount of suffering before death mercifully released the victim. At war dances the brave would boast of his exploits and took tremendous pride in those which were the most brutal and daring, so that the sobiquet "savage" was not so far amiss, after all, as applied to the Indian of primitive days.

After his first exploit on the war path, the young warrior was considered a finished product of red manhood, a valorous defender of his people.

Now let us discuss the usually attractive but never similar designs on the Blood or Blackfoot tepee. The Indian was a very superstitious person and a confirmed believer in things supernatural, such as ghosts, spirits, and dreams, to which latter belief the painting of special designs on tepees is attributed.

Ages ago, legend tells us, all the designs painted on these lodges originated in the dreams. Let us suppose, for example, that an Indian dreamed that an individual approached him and, pointing to a painted tepee, said: "My son, I am making you a present of the design on my tepee." The dreamer, on awaking, would proceed to embellish his lodge with the design which his dream benefactor has bestowed upon him. This was the tradition of my people regarding the origin of the decorated lodges.

In more recent years, there is another course which an aspiring Indian householder (if the term may be permitted) may take in order to procure a design. He first presents the owner of the design in which he is interested with a pipeful of tobacco, thereby indicating his desire to buy and use the design. If the possessor decides to sell, he lights up, and prospective buyer and seller seal the bargain with a few friendly puffs. The lodge proprietor then summons all nearby owners of painted lodges to a sacred ceremony. After each has chanted his individual tepee song, the disposing proprietor paints the purchaser's face and teaches him his tepee song, for both facial decoration and song are sacred to each lodge design and are as individual as the design itself. After the ceremony is over, remuneration takes place, all of the buyer's friends and relatives donating to assist in making the payment. Then he may paint his lodge with the design at any time he wishes. No other may copy it on any tepee without the above formality, each pattern being individually owned. These designs are never inherited by surviving relatives of a deceased owner; usually some person outside the family is sold the rights.

There is one other type of tepee which should be mentioned. These bear the decorations which are old warriors' own pictures, painted by themselves, depicting their meritorious deeds in battle. Some of these drawings or paintings date back for centuries.

Perhaps it would not be out of place here to state a few of the activities and ethics of my people during their everyday lives.

The male Indian, in his nomadic state, was above reproach in regard to his relatives of the opposite sex. His moral attitude toward them was very high. He did not indulge in any unseemly or filthy language in the presence of women. He was not allowed to intermarry; indeed, it was held very wrong to even contemplate such a thing, and dancing with women relatives was strictly forbidden. A rigidly enforced rule was that each man must do all his courting in public. Thus he was not sub-

Blood woman scraping a hide

jected to the prolonged osculatory temptations before having
the "knot tied."

Another successful custom was the separation, immediately
following marriage, of the groom from his newly-acquired
mother-in-law. Many a time I have witnessed a mother-in-law
making a hasty exit through a window, or any other quickly
accessible opening, on the approach of her son-in-law. I told
this to a pale-faced friend once and, with a wistful look, he
said "What a situation! If it could only happen to me once!"
I am unable to explain the origin of this custom, but the practice still prevails among some families.

The Indian man's attitude towards his wife was certainly
not one where he considered her his "better half" unless,
indeed, it applied to doing a great deal better than half the
labour. She was the household drudge, in the strictest sense of
the word. For his bravery and industry while engaged as a
warrior, the Indian was without a peer. But his gallantry was
discarded with his war feathers when he re-entered his tepee.
The hunt or the fight over, he would not even award personal
attention to his horses, a young single man being engaged for
that purpose. And to his wife fell all the home duties—hauling
water, chopping wood, cooking, cleaning, sewing, repairing,
etc. Before the wagon era, the firewood was hauled sometimes
long distances in large bundles on the backs of the poor women.

This was stopped by one of the Indian Agents during his tenure of office.

As an example of what the man expected of his wife, I might cite her attention to his ablutions. She had, at one time, to wash his face and comb his hair as carefully as she would for her youngest child. Another attention demanded by the husband (and still is by some of the less acculturated) was the partial undressing of his person before retiring, with particular regard to the removal of his moccasins.

The rapidly changing attitude [i.e. in 1936] of Indian women to these servile duties is perhaps best illustrated by an amusing experience of my own. Partly in jest, though possibly with a faint hope of exerting my masculine dignity, I once suggested to my "better half" that she take off my moccasins. Forthwith she seized the broom, rather than my footgear, and ere I could beat a hasty retreat she managed to get in a very telling barrage.

Shot Both Sides, head chief of the Blood tribe from 1913 to 1956. This, and the other portraits in the following pages, were taken by T. J. Hileman in 1927.

Goodstriker

Eagle Child

Heavy Shield

Mike Oka

Black Plume

Calf Robe

Running Coyote

Heavy Forehead

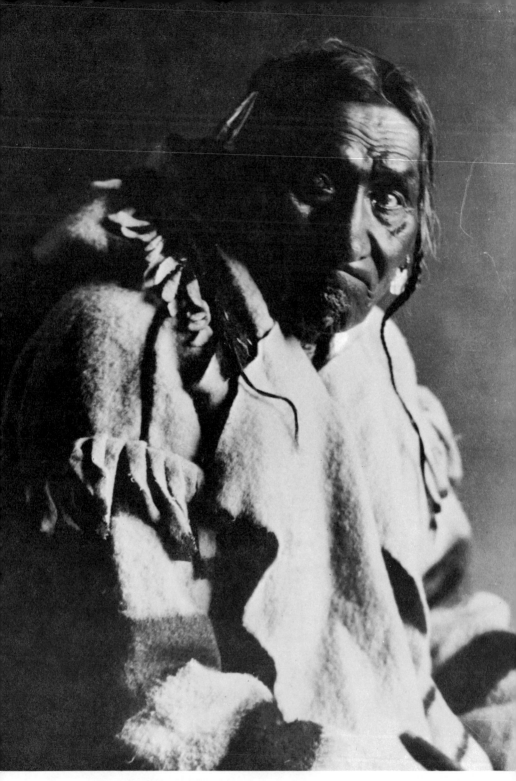

Running Sun

White Wolf

Many Mules

Big Wolf

Three Guns

CHAPTER SIX

The Great Battle

I HAVE MUCH pride in relating the following story of the Tigers of the Plains—the Blackfoot Confederacy.

The last of our battles of any importance was fought in the year 1870, when the Blackfoot Confederacy was decimated by the dreadful scourge of smallpox. Hearing of this misfortune, their enemies, the Crees, under the leadership of Chief Piapot, decided to raid them.

The Crees followed the river, starting west near Medicine Hat. At a point eighteen miles north-east of Lethbridge, the head chief of this small army had a dream which seemed to predict ill fortune for the raiders. Iron Horn, a Cree Indian who later lived at Belknap Agency in Montana, was a participant in this war expedition, and although only ten at the time, he remembered the war council that he witnessed between Piapot and his men. An Indian chief addressing any of his followers calls them his "children." On this particular morning, according to Iron Horn, the chief harangued his men in somewhat the following words: "My children, I had a dream last night. I saw a buffalo bull with iron horns goring, stamping, and killing us. We were unable to destroy it. After long meditation, I have come to the conclusion that we must abandon this venture and return home. Otherwise, misfortune awaits us."

His words had the effect of dividing the party. The more superstitious decided to return home, while the remaining warriors were prevailed upon by an opposing chieftain to continue their westward trek. "My children," this chieftain shouted, "don't believe in a dream. Advance and capture the Blackfoot nations—womenfolk and children. The smallpox killed off most of their fighters, so we won't be opposed by any great numbers."

It was decided to send ahead a reconnoitring party of Crees. These scouts were always the most essential part of an Indian war party going into a hostile country. Able-bodied young men were allotted to this special task which comprised investigating the country ahead, locating enemy camps, hunting parties, or any hostile enemy scouts.

On this occasion the scouts discovered a Blackfoot camp at Many Ghosts, the old name for the area around Fort Whoop-up. Thinking to kill two birds with one stone, they captured some of the Blackfoot ponies and reported back to the main camp. In reality these men had located only the central part of a large camp which extended to what is now called Whitney's Crossing, south of Whoop-up, and as far north as Fort Kipp.

Night was chosen as the most propitious time for making the attack. After the warriors had made the short journey to Fort Whoop-up, they discovered that Chief Mountain was head of the camp located by the Cree scouts. Deploying for action, the Crees now sent forward some of their most intrepid braves who in loud voices announced to the sleeping Blackfoot "We are here," at the same time commencing a barrage on the camp.

The place of action was at a point where the old railway bridge crossed into the Blood Reserve at St. Mary's, near Lethbridge. Some of the Blackfoot women swam across the river to the main camp, to summon aid. One of these women showed remarkable bravery by slaying four Cree warriors with her only weapon, a tomahawk, during the first part of the hostilities. Casualties were few at first. Although outnumbered, the Blackfoot held their own, due chiefly to the modern firearms which they used. The noise of rifle firing and the howling of dogs soon brought assistance to the handful of isolated Blackfoot. At break of day warriors from the Blackfoot camps north and south could be seen approaching on horseback, in twos and threes, over hills and knolls, chanting their war songs in anticipation of battle. The Cree braves, noticing these horsemen, cried out to the others: "Look at them coming over every hill. We are outnumbered. Let us retreat!"

The invaders began to retreat, the Blackfoot warriors in full pursuit. The Crees endeavored to reach the present site of the city of Lethbridge but were headed off by their enemies to a coulee south of the railway bridge at Lethbridge, near Ashcroft mine. All along the route of retreat, hand to hand conflicts occurred, and dead bodies were strewn, as the Crees tried to make a stand. If one stands on a knoll, later used by the City of Lethbridge as a dumping ground, one can see the historic landmark where Chief Piapot's warriors put up a stubborn resistance.

After throwing down large boulders on the Cree braves and killing a few in this manner, the Confederacy fighters closed in and routed them out of the coulee, sending them down a steep cutbank into the river. Here a fearful massacre occurred, the water of the river turning crimson with blood.

Calf Shirt, already wounded in the neck and arm, with arrows sticking out of his body, dispatched two of the enemy with his Bowie knife. Jerry Potts, famous interpreter for the Mounted Police in later years, did magnificent fighting for the Confederacy warriors in this battle. Referring to it in later years, Jerry said "You could shut your eyes and hit a Cree." Stabbing and drowning were the order of the day. Prairie Chicken, a Blood warrior, jumped his horse from a cutbank into the river to go after the enemy, south of where Ashcroft mine now operates.

Approximately ten Crees survived this battle in the river and crossed safely on the other side, just south of where the C.P.R. bridge now stands, where they proceeded to entrench themselves in the brush. The remains of this trench could be seen up to a few years ago. These surviving Crees had only one old revolver and no ammunition, as their supply of powder was wet from the encounter in the river. One casualty occurred in this trench, a Cree shooting another brave accidentally with his arrow.

This battle, as stated before, originated with the Crees, who went on the offensive mainly for pillaging purposes. Unfortunately for them, they came in contact with the whole Confederacy encampment and were nearly wiped out. Many of those who escaped succumbed to their wounds on the way home, only a few surviving to tell the tale.

CHAPTER SEVEN

Religion

F ROM MY ASSOCIATIONS with other races, I have come to the conclusion that the Indians of this continent take their religion in a very serious way. The majority of the Indian youth have no other alternative than to embrace the religion of the white man as taught in their schools. But our parents, and other older members of our respective tribes, still adhere to many of their ancient beliefs. When missionaries first introduced amongst my people a religion foreign to their established beliefs, they frequently encountered a very hostile reception. Very often a religious service would be interrupted by a dubious congregation.

I remember distinctly an incident that happened about 1893, during the progress of a church service conducted in the Indian tongue by one of the first missionaries to our reserve. The minister was speaking from a special passage in the Bible, dealing with the realm of his satanic majesty, with its enormous everlasting fire reserved for evil-doers, when suddenly one old fellow named Berry Child jumped to his feet and, turning to the assembly, cried, "Someone tell this white man he's a dog-faced liar!" Everybody in the room burst out laughing. Their merriment temporarily drowned the preacher's voice, but at last he proved himself equal to the occasion by informing Berry Child that he would not go "up there," pointing upwards, if he did not believe in God. Berry Child, not to be outdone, replied, "Well, let me know when you get ready to go 'up there' (Berry Child pointed upwards with his finger) so I can hang onto your shirt tail."

The incident is a typical one, showing in a pronounced way the belligerent attitude maintained by my people toward a religion foreign to their belief. Why was it that some Indians were so reluctant to discard their own faith for what they considered a very complicated foreign religion? First let me state that the Indian was a very religious individual, praying sincerely at all times. If he was ignorant of the Creator of all things, to whom then did he make his supplications? Prayers were mostly offered to the Sun, for without its presence this universe could not function. It manifests itself to us day after day, enabling every living creature on earth to enjoy the benefits of its beautiful radiance.

I once heard an argument between a missionary of the gospel and a confirmed Indian sun worshipper.

"I cannot begin to understand this God you are preaching about," said the Indian, "because we never see Him in any shape or form. What would happen to this world if my God up there," pointing in the direction of the sun, "were to get angry and refuse to supply any more light? We must have light to enable us to live."

So strongly has heliolatry been instilled into the minds of the Indians that some of the ex-pupils from Indian missionary schools reverted to this ancient belief of their grandfathers.

Now let me give an example of an Indian's prayer:

> *Help me, Sun, to live a long and prosperous life with my family and relatives. Let no harm or sickness come upon us. Pity me and hear my prayer.*

It will be noted that the entreaties of an Indian's prayer are devoted entirely to his earthly existence. He does not seek to have his sins forgiven, neither does he beseech any deity to make of him a righteous person, so that he may be eligible for the abode of the blessed, because that principle is foreign to his belief. He believes that there is only one specific Hereafter, where all Indians, irrespective of how they have conducted themselves during their sojourn on earth, will go. This Hereafter is called by them the "Big Sands."

The Indians also have believed for ages in the existence of a Supreme Being whom they designate as Napi, but I never remember hearing any of my people praying to this deity.

The Indian does not offer his prayers entirely to the Sun. Living creatures of every description are included in his daily devotions, though he doesn't pray to these in the light of a Supreme Being. Far from it.

One day I was walking with my aunt along the foot of a high cut bank where hundreds of swallows were flying about. I could see them hopping in and out of their numerous nests, from some of which the young ones were peeking. My aunt was walking a few yards ahead of me when she suddenly halted and turned around. Seizing my right arm, she began to pray, her words evidently directed to the birds:

> *Pity me, for my children's sake, you wonderful birds. Give me your power of wisdom in rearing young ones. Help my children to grow into strong, healthy men and women.*

It will be noticed that there is no mention of sins to be forgiven or of living a righteous life so as to be eligible for heaven. Foremost in her mind was her love for her offspring, for whom she prayed that they may mature into strong health men and women. She prayed to these birds for wisdom in the matter of raising children because in this case the love of my aunt for her children was so abundant that she would seek advice in the rearing of them from any source available. She observed these swallows feeding their young. She realized that these young would soon grow into fine, strong birds. My aunt, being a mother of nature, was only seeking aid from another mother of nature in the matter pertaining to the rearing of young ones. We Indians believe that birds, beasts and reptiles can feel and perceive as does man. Similar prayers are offered to different animals. But the Sun is held above all others as having power to assist mankind in most ways.

Another form of worship practised among my people relates to the good luck buffalo stone or *iniskim*. Its origin is in the story of a woman gathering firewood near a river, many years ago. While searching in the thicket this woman heard another woman singing in a very beautiful voice. The words of her song were: "Pick me up and you will be blessed with good luck through all the ages." Ascertaining the direction from whence the voice came, she started in search of the strange singer. After looking for some time she again heard the lovely voice and gazing once more, she finally located the spot, where she found a stone in the shape of a human being. "Take me now so you and your children will be favoured with good luck for all ages to come," the stone told her after she had picked it up. The woman repaired to her tepee and told of the strange event. Thus began the buffalo stone, which was to become such an important factor in the religion of my people. It was always given a prominent place in a tepee, and is still to be seen in many homes on our reserve, where it sits in a box filled with earth at the back of the house facing the entrance. A small square space, devoid of grass, is reserved for this sacred stone. This square is also used for burning sacred incense. Its sanctity is held very high. No one dares to walk in front of it, for it is considered a sanctuary and must be treated with the same respect as is an altar in church. If one entered the tepee of a noted Indian, he would immediately observe a small square facing the entrance, behind the fireplace. It usually had a little heap of ashes in its centre with three or four small rocks painted with dull red paint, placed in a row on one side.

The buffalo stone is shaped with four small bulges on one side of it, two of which represent its arms and the other two its legs. It is a rare specimen of rock and is seldom found. Its chief purpose is to bring luck to its owner in all his dealings, and he treats it with great respect. In the morning an old Indian would be heard chanting sacred songs in his tepee, offering devotions to the spirits. The buffalo stone would always be included in these prayers. The devotee would pick it up and smear it afresh with red sacred paint. While doing this he would offer a prayer for its assistance in bringing him numerous presents and good fortune for the rest of his days.

So great was the faith and respect of an Indian for the buffalo stone that one minor chief named Running Wolf used to adorn the head of his particular stone with a little toy straw hat, for fear that it might catch cold. One day a young Blood named Flying About, more or less intoxicated, entered the lodge of Running Wolf. After showing his friendliness by treating the chief to some of his 'fire water,' Flying About asked permission to give a drink to the sacred hat-clad stone. Running Wolf consented, at the same time extolling his guest for the fine unselfish spirit which prompted such an offer. Flying About then poured a good stiff drink and holding it out to the stone, addressed it as follows: "Help me, *Iniskim*. Bring

Running Wolf, a minor chief of the Bloods

me luck. Here is a drink for you." But, on second thought, he returned the cup to his own lips and drained its contents, murmuring as he did so, "Oh, he can go to town and get his own booze." Furious at this insult to his good luck stone, Running Wolf cursed the young man and told him that he was a bad boy and that when he died he was going to that place reserved for bad white men. Not content with this, he grabbed Flying About by his coat collar and threw him out of the house.

Such is the religion of my people. We pray earnestly and sincerely to whatever spirit we wish to supplicate for assistance in bestowing a special favor. We do not ask forgiveness of sins or for moral or spiritual strength to live a righteous life, so that we may be numbered among the chosen few who will be favoured with golden crowns and harps in the Hereafter.

When we entered the new era and discarded our old faith for that of a foreign race, we offered our devotions to the new Deity with the same earnest spirit as was possessed by our forefathers. We do not go to church for the purpose of scrutinizing the new styles in dress, or hearing the latest gossip. We do not make the House of God a hat show or a style parade. Our minds are on what we go to church for, and that is to worship the Creator who controls the destinies of men.

The Sun Dance originated among my people long before the advent of the white race. It is an annual tribal ceremony held in the summertime to propitiate the Sun and other lesser spirits.

The initial stages of celebrating a Sun Dance take the form of a vow made to the Sun on behalf of a relative, stricken down with a severe illness. A woman of chaste character will publicly voice her vow when the need arises, in somewhat the following words:

> I will officiate and put up a Sun Dance lodge
> next summer as a request to the Divine Powers
> for a quick recovery from illness of my relative.

After this avowal is annunciated throughout her tribe, she begins to accumulate buffalo tongues, those of each animal killed being appropriated. These delicacies are cut into large slabs, dried and boiled by women of her tribe.

No woman of questionable character may assist in handling this meat, because it is to be taken as sacred food at a great

Framework of the Blood Sun Dance lodge, 1893

public communion celebrated during the Sun Dance. All these women are first required to openly declare themselves as having lived an upright and chaste life. If one is found to be of questionable character, she is immediately disqualified and is not even allowed to remain in the sacred lodge.

The period during which the rites are performed in the Sun Dance woman's tepee, previous to any ceremonies in the main lodge, is approximately four days. The woman must abstain from food and water during this period of prayer. At intervals she is given water, colored with white clay, in an oyster shell, to moisten her tongue. If during this period the woman drinks any further water to quench her thirst, her action will bring on inclement weather during the remaining period of the Sun Dance.

The framework of the Sun Dance lodge is divided into several sections somewhat similar to a horse corral. Each of these sections consists of two long forked posts and a couple of other poles, one a little longer than the other.

The task of chopping down and hauling these posts is placed in the hands of minor chiefs, or some other responsible persons. After these saplings are cut and hauled, a couple of post holes are dug in the place selected and the straight ends of the forked posts are placed therein and tampered down. This accomplished, the shorter pole is placed crosswise on top of the two forked posts, which tends to hold them securely in place. The longer pole is then propped up against the cross pole. This is only one section completed. Others are done in a similar manner, and after completion of the whole, the finished framework resembles a high circular horse corral.

Then follows the ceremony of selecting the centre pole by the secret Horn Society. The task of selecting a tree for this purpose is placed in charge of two able warriors who proceed on horseback to the nearby thickets, and after making their selection, and placing a mark thereon, they report back to the main body.

The Horn Society, dressed in their best beaded regalia, and accompanied by their women members, then proceed to the designated spot. At approximately 200 yards from their destination, a halt is called. Four renowned and able warriors are chosen from those present to go forward to make a final official discovery of the tree already selected, advancing, single file, into the woods. These men imitate a kit fox's howl, to indicate that they have discovered the marked tree. On hearing this, everybody, including the women members, begins to sing to beat the drums. The four men who made the final selection now appear running to and fro in single file as they emerge from the woods. As they run they circle once, to signify that they have located their objective. Coming to a halt about 25 yards from the main body, each man alternately kicks and scatters with his feet a conglomeration of sticks and buffalo chips heaped in front of the members standing in a row. At this point another warrior from the ranks asks them for news. But before they utter a word to him, he must relate in a loud voice any heroic achievements credited to him in his youth. After this, he turns to the four for instructions concerning details of the tree's location, and on being informed acquaints the others with this information. The four men then relate their individual war achievements, how they led war parties in former days, and how they are now going to lead the Horn Society to their destination. After these ceremonies, everyone approaches the tree on foot and, on arriving at their destination, all sit down. A fire is kindled by a member chosen especially for this task. He alone is authorized to ignite the fire, light the pipes used for smoking, and burn the incense. No matches are used for lighting the pipes.

At this point, a member will fill his pipe and offer it to one of the wise old men in attendance, requesting him to pray that he may have good luck in his various undertakings and bring up his children properly. The patriarch then takes the pipe and, holding the stone bowl in his right hand and pointing upward with the stem, prays for every member present, and for the whole tribe in general.

At the conclusion of this prayer everyone responds by

saying "Hey," which signifies "Amen." Then the patriarch returns the pipe to the man who offered it to him, who lights it from the fire and offers it to each member separately. Each member takes four puffs at it, at the same time stroking the donor's body twice on either side. After this, four sweetgrass incenses are lighted at the base of the chosen tree, each burning at one of the four points of the compass. During the lighting of this incense everyone present prays that the tree may fall in an easterly direction; if not, that it may strike the ground pointing west, and that all branches may remain intact as the tree falls. If any limbs of the tree break off while falling, it will denote ill luck for some member of the society officiating at the ceremony. Should the tree fall in a northerly or southerly direction, a death in the family of someone officiating is indicated.

After the first four incenses have died out, another four are lighted. The senior Horn member then picks up two axes for use in felling this tree. These he consecrates by holding each one separately over the smoke of an incense. He selects two able-bodied members from those present, instructing each to kneel beside an incense, those on the north and south sides being indicated. While these two members are kneeling, he orders them to pray for protection from harm while chopping down the tree, and to include in their request a long and happy life with their families. The assembly remains silent during the progress of these supplications. When completed, the warrior picks up one of the axes and holding it for a moment over the fumes of an incense, hands it to one of the kneeling men. He does the same thing with the other axe, handing it to the other kneeling man. Now, kneeling himself, his right hand on the base of the tree, he prays as follows:

> *Dweller of Above, who gave us Indians the ceremony of Sun Dance, I pray you to help us at this time and use your divine power in guarding this tree so as not to break any of its branches when it strikes the ground.*

After this short invocation, he arises and requests the lighter to ignite all four incenses. He then instructs his companions with the axes to arise. Approaching first the one standing due south, he grasps the man's arms below the elbows and makes four moves as if chopping down a tree. At each alternative move, the axe is held over the sacred smoke. This performance is repeated by the other member standing opposite. After these ceremonies the actual chopping begins, and while the work is in progress all members are requested to pray.

If the tree falls in an easterly or westerly direction it is utilized. If it strikes the ground contrary to these directions it is abandoned and a new one is selected for the purpose. A tree never strikes the ground with terrific force because it is never chopped right off, but is allowed to fall gradually. While swaying in mid-air everybody present must shout continuously until it falls. It is then trimmed, peeled, and hauled to camp at the head of a huge procession, where it is unloaded to await further ceremony.

On the fourth day of her fasting, the Sun Dance woman changes her abode to a temporary canopy erected in close proximity to the frame structure intended for the Sun Dance lodge. Everybody in camp assembles nearby and sits down in a large circle. Numerous skin bags filled with buffalo tongue, already consecrated and cut into small pieces, are opened and put out in a prominent place. At this point a number of women, all of whom have dedicated themselves on a previous occasion for a similar purpose, will approach the bags of buffalo tongue, and each will pick up a piece of meat. Holding it in her hand she must openly declare herself, before the huge assembly, to be living a virtuous life, relating instances where temptations have been placed in her way by young tribesmen whom she will name in a loud voice. Needless to say, these ardent swains will be conspicuous by their absence during these avowals, and when they do appear, the other men will have a hearty laugh at their expense.

Centre pole being raised at the Blood Sun Dance, 1893

After this public avowal some of the men distribute morsels of sacred tongue to everyone present, including the children, and on receiving their portions each must pray before eating this hieratic food.

Now let us turn our attention to a couple of green hides placed inside the frame pole structure intended for a Sun Dance lodge. Two warriors will mingle with the great assembly and, at an opportune time, they will seize two members thereof, either man, woman or child. The persons must accompany the warriors before a gathering of old men sitting beside the green hides, where incense is burning. These two persons are required to cut the green hides into strips, but before doing so they must purchase this privilege from the persons who performed a similar task at the previous Sun Dance. Their faces are painted the same color as were the faces of the previous cutters. Then a warrior will relate his deeds of valor—those accomplished with a knife being especially mentioned—after which an old man will hand each candidate a knife and, grasping one by both hands, will go through with an affectation of cutting. Alternately the knife is held over the smoke of incense, and at the fourth move a split is made into the hide, when actual cutting begins.

Every strip is cut a certain length and is placed on top of a cross pole of the framework of logs. Next, a large bundle of brush wood is tied securely at the forked end of a huge pole, which is lying on the ground.

A number of men and women are now standing in pairs in a row, singing to the beating of the drums, each couple holding up before them two long poles tied together, about four feet apart at the top. Similar singing groups of men and women converge from all directions on the framework of poles. The Sun Dance woman's husband squats on the brush tied on the pole, flapping his blanket, and imitating the noise of an eagle by whistling through a bone. Then, amidst loud clamor and great applause the huge pole is gradually raised. When the top is some feet off the ground the man on the brush jumps off. The long poles carried by the singing groups are now used to propel the big pole vertically into place. When this task is accomplished, various Indians carrying articles of sacrifice and medicine pipes filled with tobacco, approach the Sun Dance couple; they offer them a smoke, and give them any articles that they wish to sacrifice, at the same time requesting their prayers. The sacred couple pray and tie all offerings to the upper end of every large rafter pole. These

Singing happy songs, the Bloods bring green branches for the Sun Dance lodge, 1907.

long poles are then propelled into their places, their small ends converging at the forked end of the centre pole. Their larger ends are tied on the cross poles with the rawhide thongs. Now the framework is complete. The couple officiating at the initial stage retire to their tepee; their task is completed. The lodge is up and ready for use.

The next morning great excitement prevails in the huge encampment. Young boys riding bareback on their galloping ponies may be seen driving herds of horses into camp. Head dresses and buckskin suits of magnificent workmanship are hung on tripods to air them. Old warriors walking around the camp call out loudly to everyone to hurry. On this day one of the most spectacular sights of the Sun Dance takes place. Hundreds of Indians in all their finery, parade to a nearby wood to bring back tree branches to be used as covering for their Sun Dance lodge. Different societies and lodges, mounted and dressed in gorgeous attire, are represented in this body, while unattached Indians ride in small groups to join in this annual parade. When they have reached their objective, all are supplied with foliage, and a monster parade forms at the outskirts of the woods and starts on its return journey to camp, each rider dragging a limb of a tree on his rope. Amidst loud singing and shouting the spectacular parade wheels inside the encampment, some persons firing shots in the air as they enter. Sometimes two or three such trips are necessary before a sufficient supply of foliage is obtained to cover the huge framework of poles in the centre of the encampment. After this is done, everything is ready for a day of ceremony and war dancing.

Different lodges and societies now take over the ceremonies. There were eight different Indian societies functioning at one of these Sun Dances when I was a boy. The great secret Horn Society was the senior lodge; next came the Eagle Society; third, Black Police; fourth, Dogs; fifth, Flies; sixth, Crazy Dogs; seventh, Pigeon Society; eighth, the woman's lodge, which I will call the Buffaloes. Any two of these societies could officiate at a day's ceremonies. Their rites consist chiefly of dances.

The leader of each society detailed to officiate at a day's ceremonies will select about six affluent members to participate with him. Members thus selected don their best beaded regalia and assemble in rows on the edges of the tepees, singing at intervals their society songs. Each man is armed with a rifle and is supplied with a belt of ammunition which he wears around his waist. The other society detailed for this purpose repeats this performance in another direction. These two small groups converge on the Sun Dance lodge at intervals, singing as they do so. On arrival there, each group enters and sits facing each other. Their relatives, staggering under huge bundles of dry goods, also approach the great lodge. These goods are to be given away as presents to visitors. Other women carrying refreshments, such as large pails of boiled meat, broth of varied ingredients, and hundreds of slabs of fried bread, also make their appearance.

When everybody is assembled in the lodge, the old warriors begin to sing and drum. Then the two groups of lodge members jump to their feet and start a rhythmical movement, accompanied by yells and women's war chants. Several shots are also fired into the air by these participants. Women relatives— mothers, wives, sisters—rush up to dance beside a relative, making a "La, La, La!" noise with their tongues. This is called "assisting." Before any person can assist a relative, he or she will have to pay by placing goods such as blankets, shawls, or anything else, on the ground beside the person to be assisted. These goods are collected into a heap, to be given to visiting tribesmen as presents. Sometimes horses are tendered as payments for assisting relatives. These are then led to the entrance of the lodge and taken away by their new owners.

Another important figure in these ceremonies is a warrior dancing at an entrance to the Sun Dance lodge during the progress of the other dance. This is a selected place reserved for a lone survivor of a skirmish or a man reputed to have dispatched an enemy. Considerable payment is required of those who dance in this honoured place. Horses and goods are lavishly given away by these dancing warriors.

After this first dance, refreshments are served. At one Sun Dance I remember sitting down to receive my portion of refreshments. My mother had had the foresight to make me carry a large bowl. A big six-foot warrior, with a pail of crushed chokecherry broth, approached me first. I held out my bowl; he tipped his pail, emptied about half a pint of broth into it, and moved on. A few seconds later another fellow came along with a pail of rice. Some of this was spilled over my crushed chokecherry broth. The next gentleman had boiled beans, some of which he emptied into my already half-filled bowl. The fourth individual had evaporated peaches in his pail, a portion of which was added to my mulligan. The last man filled my bowl to overflowing with an additional helping of dried apples.

I placed this epicurian puzzle in front of me, trying to find the best way out of my dilemma. Having no spoon, I started picking out the evaporated peaches with my fingers. While thus engaged, two fellows placed a large pan filled with boiled meat in front of me. On receiving a chunk of meat on one corner of his blanket, each Indian would grunt like a hog rooting in the ground. When I received my chunk of meat on the end of my blanket, I grunted and decided to call it a day. My appetite being unequal to the mixture in my bowl, I emptied it into a gopher hole on my way to my father's tepee.

After refreshments dancing is again resumed. This time warriors relate tales of heroic achievements, accompanied by a pantomimic display of skirmishes in which they had participated in their youth. Scores of men take part in this sham fight, each participant making a considerable payment before being allowed to do so.

Other ceremonies, too numerous to mention, take place during this period of prayer and fun. Suffice it to say that we enjoy this annual celebration, with all its attendant festivities.

CHAPTER EIGHT

Medicine Men

I HAVE FREQUENTLY been asked, "How did the Indian give medical attention to fellow tribesmen who were in ill health, before the advent of modern medical science?"

I will now endeavour to answer this question.

Outside of the sketchy accounts of the medicine man and his chantings given in history books, very little has been written on this subject. Being a full-blooded native myself, who has resided with, and seen, medicine men ministering to their ailing patients, and having been administered to myself for minor physical ailments by these Indian doctors, I feel that I am in a position to speak with some authority on the subject.

Ages ago, when an Indian desired to obtain further knowledge along medical lines, he would retire for several days to some secluded place selected by himself. High, prominent landscapes were usually chosen for this purpose. First, he would erect a canopy, building it with sticks covered with foliage, the size of canopy being large enough to shelter a fairly large sized man, with interior space just sufficiently high for the devotee to crawl into on his hands and knees when retiring at night. A large flat rock served as a covering for the door space. For four days an Indian in such seclusion would abstain from food and water, spending his time in beseeching the spirits to hear his entreaties. At times he would cry out in a loud lamenting voice for the purpose of arousing the sympathy of a local spirit, so that he might be gifted with a special power or knowledge, according to his wishes. At the end of that time food and water would be brought by relatives and set out in a prominent place where he could get them, for he must not be disturbed during his meditations and prayers.

During his seclusion, a spirit taking the form of an animal or a bird would approach the Indian in a dream. "My son, why are you in solitude?" this dream visitor would ask. "Because I crave for knowledge and power to enable me to render medical attention," the Indian would reply. The spirit would then pronounce a benediction upon the young man, somewhat in the following words:

> I will have compassion upon you, my son. Your request shall be granted. I will endow you with abundant wisdom. You shall be a great doctor among your people. Many ponies and much property will come your way.

After the benediction he would show the student many different varieties of herbs and roots which he must use in his newly acquired profession as a medicine man. A sacred chant would also be taught to the novice by his dream benefactor. This song he had to memorize so as to sing it when in attendance upon a sick person. Thus we have the origin of the medicine man's weird chanting.

Having come into his "medicine," the Indian would return to his people next morning. At the first opportune time he would make himself available as a medicine man, administering to those who were in need of his services.

But not all aspirants were successful in obtaining knowledge in this mysterious way. A story is told of a certain warrior who went into seclusion for the purpose of gaining special wisdom as a medicine man. He was not as fortunate as some, for a real live bear, instead of a spirit, came and devoured him. When his immediate family brought food on the fourth day, they found nothing left of him but a few bones.

Another fellow tied himself on a raft to commune with the spirits. After being pushed out to float, he was never seen again. He too sacrificed his life in his search for wisdom.

When the medicine man's diagnosis of a case showed the ailment to be internal, he would resort to his large herbarium for a remedy. The dried herbs selected for his patient were boiled first, then transfused and the sediment discarded. Sometimes other ingredients were used. Some employed a dried root which was ground into a fine powder. This was added to the solution and was ready for use when cool.

All medicine men did not use the same herbs for special ailments; each had his own assortment of therapeutic herbs which were numerous and varied. His knowledge and skill in the use of them was amazing.

For a person suffering from a feeling of lassitude, accompanied by frequent nose bleed and headache, the following treatment was given: The medicine man drove a wooden picket, about two feet long, into the ground, leaving about a foot and a half sticking up. The patient then knelt with his left arm and knee alongside this picket, gripping it at the top with his right hand, the arm of which was bare to the shoulder. The attending medicine man then started to work the tips of his fingers on the patient's body, pressing toward the right arm. Next, he tied a tourniquet midway between the shoulder and elbow and an attending medicine man took a flint knife and made an incision into an artery on the inside of this arm, at the elbow joint. Blood would squirt out in a long red stream, sometimes to a distance of three or four feet. After enough blood had been drained from this portion of the patient's arm below the tourniquet, a solution of herbs was placed over the incision. The patient was then required to hold his forearm in an upright position against his shoulder for a short time. The bleeding stopped immediately; no bandages were required for this treatment and the results obtained were often very satisfactory. I witnessed this being done on several occasions when in my teens. Persons who underwent this treatment never, to the best of my knowledge, suffered from any ill aftereffects.

A much more painful operation performed by Indian medicine men was what white doctors call "wet cupping." I have numerous scars on my breast as a result of this operation.

In this operation the medicine man began by feeling all over his patient's body with the tips of his fingers. "Here it is," he would presently say, indicating a spot which was sensitive to the touch and perhaps feverish and palpitating. Having located the offending spot, he then used his only surgical instrument, the flint knife, and made an incision. He then applied his lips to the wound and, as he sucked the blood he spit it out, as is done in cases of rattlesnake bites. Beneficial results were always obtained from this treatment, chronic complaints often disappearing entirely.

I was subjected to the above treatment as a baby and as an adult. I always felt 100 per cent strong at the spot where these scars still showed on my breast.

A less painful way of treating a sore spot was to burn thorn needles stuck into a patient's skin. These burrs were so placed as to cover the spot complained of. They were then ignited. Some would throw out considerable sparks as soon as the flames were applied to them. Those were the ones doing a patient the most good. Others burned right down to the skin without throwing out one spark. These had to be pressed down on the surface of the skin before anyone could attain the desired benefit from this treatment.

Now let us see what was done for a person suffering from a very severe cold. Take a round smooth rock weighing about five pounds; pinkish colored ones were preferable because they throw more heat and do not break asunder. Now grease this rock and put it into the fire until it is red hot. Next have your patient ready stripped to his waist and covered with a blanket. Get a basin half full of water and mix with it some sweet grass. Take your rock out of the fire and immediately roll it into the basin already half full of water. As soon as the steam starts to rise, have your patient bend over it, using his blanket as a covering. Do not let any steam escape. A patient should remain in that position until the rock is incapable of throwing out any more heat, when a towel is handed to him for the purpose of wiping his perspiring face and body. This is a sure cure for a very bad cold.

Rheumatic pains were treated by a person continually pounding the affected spot with a porcupine tail. These tails were cut to about four inches in length. The hair was trimmed to the skin with a little of the bristle hairs, cut evenly, left on at one end. The other end served as a handle. This was a great weapon used by old rheumatic people to combat aching joints. I have so much faith in it that I have one of these little tails in my valise which I do not hesitate to use on both of my knees when the occasion arises.

CHAPTER NINE

Customs

IT IS CUSTOMARY for a Blood Indian to be dressed for interment before his demise. He is prepared for burial in his best
clothes which, if he is an affluent person, usually consist of
a buckskin suit. His hair is combed and plaited nicely, and
his face is painted when those in attendance conclude that
the end is near. Some people might say: "They must want
to get rid of their dead pretty quick." But such is not the case.
This ancient custom of dressing up a person on the point of
death is derived from the following old belief:

Upon a person's death his spirit, or "shadow" as the Indians call it, immediately takes flight from the earthly body and
journeys to the Big Sands in such clothing as is worn on the
death bed. To dress an Indian for burial after death is considered to be of no benefit to him in the hereafter, since his
"shadow" has already arrived in the spirit world. Thus, if
he were clad in a nightgown when dying, his spirit would
arrive at its destination thus attired and he would spend eter-
nity thus. Hence the very elaborate surroundings of some
wealthy man and his magnificent attire before his death.

The mourning period observed by those bereaved lasts
for a year. The women mourners sacrifice their beautiful long
hair and wear their skirts short. At intervals a visit is made to

the burial place of the deceased, where the bereaved weep and lament loudly, calling on the departed by name. I recall noticing, when a small boy, one woman in particular coming from the graveside of her offspring. That portion of her legs below the knees showed a number of long scratches crossways, and her limbs were marked like pieces of birch. I wondered how she happened to be scratched that way; I was destined to find out soon after, when my step-mother asked me to accompany her to the grave of my baby brother. On arrival there she took out a piece of glass and deliberately started to tear her skin crossways below both her knees, at the same time wailing in a loud voice for her baby. Blood flowed from these self-inflicted wounds. I tried my utmost to prevent her from following this custom, but she was adamant. Being almost a baby myself then, I could not do much, only stare and stand at a considerable distance. It was considered proper for our women to scratch their lower limbs in this manner at intervals during the period of mourning.

Another custom was the chopping off of the tip of one little finger on the death of an especially dear one. This way of showing grief, I heard, was carried out by my father and other members of the immediate family, on the death of my uncle. I did not witness the actual severing of the digits, but I saw my father's hand bandaged in a large bundle a week later and surmised that the report must have been true. This custom, however, was only carried out on rare occasions.

A minor sacrifice bereaved persons underwent was the discarding of all personal property to other Indians. I have seen Indian women walk into a bereaved person's lodge and deliberately cart away everything they could lay their hands on—pots, pans, bedding, and any food available. After others have thus helped themselves, the bereaved person is supposed to discard the remainder of his or her possessions by throwing them into the river. Custom demands that the mourner be destitute and in rags during the period of mourning.

Numerous forms of interment were used by the Bloods. In the case of a rich, influential chieftain, his tepee would be erected and furnished as for immediate occupation. Beds were made around the walls complete and a fireplace installed in the centre. Food bags were filled with eatables and placed within. On a bed facing the entrance, covered with numerous robes, was laid the corpse. After this, the exit was sewn shut and the lodge abandoned.

Another form of interment was to deposit the corpse on

the branches of trees. The cadaver was wrapped in a huge bundle and left securely tied to the branches selected for this purpose.

Soon after the establishment of my people on a reserve, they adopted a more modern form of burial by placing their dead in wooden coffins and depositing them in small shanties. One could look into these huts and see coffin upon coffin piled high within.

One ancient custom, the "making of a brave," has been so misinterpreted and criticized that I feel it my duty to explain it more fully here.

In case of the severe illness of a close relative, an Indian would make a solemn vow, usually to the Sun, in the following words: "I will sacrifice my body to you, to be lacerated, at the next Sun Dance ceremonies, trusting my relative will recover from his illness." A candidate for this ceremony would then purchase the right to carry out his vow from another Indian who had previously been through this terrible ordeal. This done, he was free to present himself at the next annual Sun Dance to be pierced.

Minus his attire, excepting his breech cloth and moccasins, his body was first plastered with white clay. A coronet of sage bush adorned his head; he also wore bracelets and anklets of the same bush. Thus attired, he paced up and down, like a caged animal, close to the centre pole of the Sun Dance lodge. He stretched his arms at intervals and sang in defiance of the torture soon to be undergone. At a given signal from attending warriors, he lay down on his back and was asked the following questions by one of the sages in attendance: "Do you wish to be pierced deeply or slightly?" If he says deeply, then he will be pierced lightly; if he says slightly, then he must suffer a deep penetration.

After this formality, an arrowhead, sharpened and greased to a razor's edge, was picked up by an old man, who held the muscle of one side of the candidate's breast out taut and pushed the arrow through it. Blood started trickling down the sides of the candidate. A small stick, sharpened at one end, was thrust through the wound and left in with both ends showing. Similar operations were performed on the opposite side. Next, he would turn over, and similar lacerations were made on his right shoulder blade and stick thrust through the wounds. Two rawhide thongs, fastened securely at one end

A member of the Blood tribe undergoes a self-torture ritual during the Sun Dance in 1894.

to the top of the centrepole, were then tied fast to both of the inserted sticks at his breast, after he regained his feet. A shield was tied to the inserted stick at his right shoulder blade.

At this moment weird chanting and drumming began, accompanied by loud applause from a number of old women. This was done to arouse excitement. The candidate then started to dance with a backward pulling motion, keeping time with the drums, and at the same time pulling full weight on the thongs attached to the sticks inserted in his breast. At intervals while dancing, he would seize the shield fastened to his shoulder blade and do his utmost, tearing his flesh, to get it loose. If he was unable to release himself from the two thongs attached to his bosom, an incision was made into the muscles holding the sticks in place, and again he must dance, taking his weight, as before, on the rawhide thongs. If this fails to release him, a spectator would grasp him from behind his shoulder and pull down on the thongs. The added weight would tear the flesh with a sickening sound, releasing both sticks and sending both men to the ground. The flesh holding the stick and shield attached to his shoulder blade was ripped from him if he failed to tear them loose after repeated efforts. This was the custom which writers described as "the making of a brave" and which they erroneously say all male Indians must submit to in order to be placed in the category of the "brave." But, as already stated, the only reason why an Indian subjected himself to this ordeal was to propitiate the Sun god for the recovery from illness of a very dear relative.

Eagle Ribs, a member of our tribe and later one of our counsellors, subjected himself to this ceremony three times in succession. A belief in dreams led Eagle Ribs to undergo this marvellous feat of endurance. One night a person appeared to him in a dream saying, "Sacrifice yourself to be pierced three days in succession at this Sun Dance if you would have your father recover." Accordingly, the next day Eagle Ribs presented himself for this painful ordeal at the Sun Dance ceremonies, and thrice went through with this painful ritual.

Other Indians who sacrificed themselves in the years immediately before this custom was officially stopped were Heavy Head, Tough Bread and Sarcee Man, the latter being a Peigan Indian.

The practice of taking the scalp from a vanquished foe was done mainly for the purpose of proving the prowess of the victor. An incision was made around the top of the head and the skin pulled off with a quick jerk. The scalp was then kept as a souvenir; at war dances it was attached to a long stick and held high in the air by the owner while dancing.

Another custom which played a prominent part in the life of a warrior on the eve of battle was to cut away a small portion of his body as an offering to any of the numerous lesser spirits then worshipped by our people.

I witnessed a revival of this custom during the great war in Europe. One evening, during those dark days of 1917 when the Germans were having things pretty much their own way, I was walking along a French road with a number of other Indian lads. We stopped at a small clearing and sat down, and after a few minutes several of the boys began to pray. Some made supplication for the success of the allies, while others prayed for a happy return to their fathers and mothers, or to their families. George Strangling Wolf, while praying, took a needle out of his "housewife" (a soldier's name for a sewing kit) and inserted it into the skin near his knee. He then took an army knife and sliced off that portion of the flesh which he was holding out taut with the needle. Pointing in the direction of the sun, and still holding the small portion of bloody flesh in his hand, George offered the following prayer:

> *Help me, Sun, to survive this terrible war, that I*
> *may meet my relatives again. With this request,*
> *I offer you my body as food.*

He then dug a small hole in the ground with his finger and buried the bloody thing he was holding. Strangling Wolf was a strong adherent to the ancient beliefs of his forefathers.

As far as I could learn, an ancient ceremony of marriage among my people was never officially supressed by the government. This ceremony was, in olden days, the Indian way of solemnizing a marriage.

When a young man arrived at the age when it was considered he should rightly marry, he was advised of the fact

Polygamy was common among the Bloods, as indicated by this man and his two wives in 1892.

by his family. His parents cast about among the marriageable maidens of his tribe for a suitable "better half," or, as is often the case now even in Indian homes, a household "combatant" for their son. The girl was consulted only on very rare occasions. If both parents of the prospective bride and groom were pleased with the match, a day was set for the wedding, and in the interval the respective parents busied themselves in preparing the new home. A new tepee was set up by the young man's parents and equipped with all the furnishings necessary to complete the Indian lodge. Horses were also given to him, in fact, everything necessary to give him a start in his matrimonial career. The young lady then presented the groom's parents with a number of beaded moccasins, worked with her own hands, and immediately took charge of the newly-prepared tepee. When the groom also moved in, they were considered man and wife. A few days later the young man and his bride paid a visit to her parents. He then tendered payment for his mate by presenting all her male relatives each with a pony. This last ceremony legally bound the marriage. Even in the case of abuse of the bride in her new home, her parents could not take her back after the paying event; the knot was tied irretrievably, legally and ceremonially.

Hospitality is instinctive among the Indians. No tribesman ever visits a tepee without being sure of a warm welcome. My own people are all associated as brothers, and no Blood is ever found "down and out," nor does he need to ask for assistance, provided he has done nothing which would cause him to be ostracized. There is no aristocracy among the tribe; one person is as good as another, and the humble are as welcome to visit the chief's home as the richest inhabitants of the reserve. The chief never dominates or intrudes in discharging the responsibilities of his position. He is a fine, staunch friend, and will stand by his friends and tribesmen to the end. But a person must be careful not to offend a chief's sense of justice or honor, for he will never forget an offence of this sort. He is as bitter an enemy as a true friend, and eventually will punish the offender, either physically or spiritually.

I have heard it said, during fairs and Indian pow-wows, "Be sure to leave nothing loose outside tonight. The Indians are in town!"

Let me say, first, that the Indians are not born thieves, though I must admit that after the coming of the white man he showed himself an apt pupil in the art of petty thieving. In olden days he took nothing that did not belong to him, with the exception of the results of his raiding excursions against hostile tribes. His spoils of war greatly enhanced his prestige. Hence, in his raids, he appropriated everything he could, not primarily for material gain, but rather, to increase his prestige among his fellow warriors. He did not drink intoxicating liquors because he never made or knew about them. He did not swear. The Blackfoot language included no profanity, and any unseemly utterances before women relatives were strictly avoided. In those days a woman who was unfaithful to her husband paid a severe penalty. She was either immediately killed or the tip of her nose was cut off, the latter action being intended to destroy her beauty.

My aunt, a woman in her 80th year when she passed away, once related to me an incident that she had witnessed when a married woman was caught in illicit ecstasy with a young man. Her husband took her to their tepee and ordered her to dress up in her best attire for burial. In the interim he sat down and immediately started to sharpen his huge hunting knife. After his wife had combed her hair and painted her face, he led her to the centre of the huge encampment, and there, in front of everyone, deliberately hacked her to death. While she lay prostrate on the ground the assassin started to walk away but, looking back at his ghastly work, he observed his wife writhing and kicking on the ground in her death agony. He then fled from this gruesome sight, crying out for her in a loud voice as he ran.

On another occasion a married woman was caught indulging in an amorous embrace with her paramour. Her husband immediately ordered her home where he proceeded to cut the cords of both her legs above the heels. Next he severed both of her ears. Not satisfied with this mutilation, the man cut the tip of her nose off. Last of all, he cut her hair close to her head and told her to go back to her sweetheart. This woman had been a great beauty. After she was thus disfigured she was unable to look anyone in the face and in her loneliness and despair she repaired to a bush and hanged herself.

The oldtime Indian had his own code of ethics and he lived up to that code. One of his customs was to purchase his wife from her parents. Such a marriage was as binding as that of any white man. After the payment was made for the young lady the parents had no more control over her.

Before they became entangled with modern methods of

civilization, the Blackfoot lived to a good old age, sometimes
past the century mark. They were also a distinctly nomadic
people, moving as they did from place to place, sometimes
at a moment's notice. As a result, they could make little or
no provision for their aged people beyond the attentions
granted by immediate relatives. The only recourse, on occasion, was to abandon these aged centenarians to their fate. In
the majority of cases the old people were so feeble that they
were incapable of walking any distance and their great age had
dimmed their eyesight. When it was decided to abandon them,
a canopy was erected wherein they sat and gradually died of
starvation.

Spear Chief, a member of the Blood tribe and quite an old
man when he told the story, related to me the following incident of his grandmother's childhood.

When a large encampment of Indians were moving to a new
location, his grandmother and some other children noticed
an old woman who had been forsaken by her family, sitting
solitary under a canopy. Being curious like all children, these
little girls ran over and gathered around the poor emaciated
crone. The centenarian looked up at them from her squatting
position and uttered a prophecy to the children around her,
which prediction has been handed down from generation to
generation. "My children," she said, "two generations from
now your great grandchildren will be living on top of wood
and all their commodities will be of iron. Every one of them
will try and be a great chief and they will leave no camp mark
when they move their camps." We are now living in that
period of time she foretold, and the interpretation of her
prediction is that my people have wooden floors in their homes
and iron is used extensively. An Indian loves self-aggrandise-
ment and wants to be a person of some importance. When
we move our tents we leave nothing but a conglomeration of
paper and cardboard boxes, which the wind blows away,
whereas the primitive Indian marked with stones the camp
site he was vacating. So the prediction of the old abandoned
woman has come true.

CHAPTER TEN

Ghosts and Spirits

LONG YEARS AGO, a small party of Bloods went on a warring expedition against their enemies who inhabited what is now known as Saskatchewan. Somewhere in the vicinity of Medicine Hat or Cypress Hills they came to a vast tract of sandy plain where their leader decided to call a halt and camp for the night. When darkness overwhelmed the prairies, these travellers heard a strange chief inviting his guests in a loud voice to come and smoke. A woman calling her child, young men singing, and dogs barking were other noises heard by this small party of men. These clamorous sounds indicated to them that they were in close proximity to a huge mysterious encampment. Soon afterwards another chief was heard crying out, "Hear me, hear me, everybody, young men and children included! Don't molest these people who have come to visit us. Let them rest in peace, so that they may continue their journey in the morning. They must not be disturbed."

"These are not real people we are hearing," the leader informed his party, his voice coming from under the buffalo robe in which he had wrapped himself, "I think we must have invaded the Big Sands."

By this time the less intrepid members of the party had begun to roll toward the older ones, clasping them tightly as the weird, mysterious voices continued throughout the night. At break of day the noises subsided and our warriors continued on their journey.

The foregoing story has been handed down from generation to generation and I narrate it merely as an example of hundreds of other ghost stories told in the tepees of my people.

As stated before, the Indian is very superstitious. He believes absolutely in the supernatural and in the existence of ghosts. Persons claiming power to commune with spirits would occasionally hold seances for the purpose of communication with a departed relative. I remember a woman of our tribe who was reputed to commune with one special person who had died a few years before. This woman's name was Medicine Pipe Woman and she was the wife of Steel.

The following incident occurred in 1911, near the old agency. I was employed at that time as handy man at St. Paul's Indian School adjacent to our reserve. Another fellow, Eagle Speaker, a firm believer in ghosts, was also employed in the same capacity. Eagle Speaker had recently lost his wife and took his bereavement very hard. One evening, after we had retired, I started a lively conversation with my friend in order to divert his mind from his recent loss. But our talk eventually drifted back to Eagle Speaker's bereavement.

"Eagle Flying," he said, addressing me by the name which I then bore, "let us go and see Medicine Pipe Woman tomorrow evening after chore time. She has power to commune with spirits. I would like to ask her to find out if my wife has returned to the husband who predeceased her."

Next evening I accompanied my friend to Mrs. Steel's tepee. After making our mission known, we presented her with little gifts of tobacco which she accepted as compensation for her trouble.

"Now keep still and remain quiet," she instructed us. "They don't like noise." This we interpreted as referring to the ghosts. She took from a small bag some dried sweetgrass and placed it on the hot embers of her fire. Immediately the interior of her tepee was diffused with a sweet scent from this plant. Mrs. Steel then began to chant a weird song in a low murmuring tone of voice. In the midst of this ghostly chanting my companion and I heard a loud whistling noise coming from one direction. The half-dead fire, throwing ghostly flickering shadows on the walls of the lodge, added an eerie atmosphere to our surroundings. At this stage a strange, spooky feeling began to creep up and down my spine and I

Eagle Speaker, seen here in the 1920s, accompanied by author to ask a holy woman about his dead wife.

could not keep still. The mysterious whistling subsided after a while and Mrs. Steel spoke as if she were addressing a newcomer.

"This boy Eagle Speaker would like to know if his wife has already returned to her former husband," she said. There was some more whistling, and when this subsided, Mrs. Steel turned to her two frightened young visitors. "My ghost says your wife has returned to her former husband," she informed my friend in a callous tone. As it was quite late by the time she was finished, we asked permission to sleep in her tepee, fearful, after our weird experience, to travel home in the dark.

Whenever I mention the above incident to my white friends they usually indulge in a hearty laugh at my expense. Our missionary, Mr. L. Wood, attempted to explain the matter in this way: "Some people have a knack of throwing their voices," he said. "Mrs. Steel must be gifted in this way." But this does not account for the mysterious noises at Mrs. Steel's lodge that night, for I was certainly in control of my normal faculties when the incident occurred.

Any unusual sound is regarded by my people as of a supernatural origin. An owl perched on a tree in close proximity to a lodge is considered an ill omen, for this bird is believed to be a person who died and is returning in the form of an owl. Dogs barking at night, their growling seeming to come from their nostrils, indicate that a ghost is approaching. A flickering blue light at a distance is thought to be a spirit walking around. A tall dark object having the appearance of floating in space is also considered to have supernatural origin. If an Indian imagines he hears his name called, he will answer, "Go by yourself." If is a common belief that a ghost is responsible and should be told to go by himself. But a ghost is not without fear, according to my people. I have been advised by friends on several occasions, while out walking at night time, to take a pliable switch and whip around with it an intervals, at the same time making a loud hooting noise. This is done to scare away any ghosts that may be in close range.

A white man with a bald head is a great protection from spirits; in fact, all white people are. I heard one spiritualist say his ghost informed him that all spirits keep at a safe distance from white people, owing to a peculiar odor which is supposed to emanate from them. Another reason is that they are not considered by ghosts to be real humans!

There is no heaven or hell for an Indian after his time on earth has expired. The spirits of Indians who lived in harmony with their neighbors while on this earth take immediate flight to their reward in the Big Sands where every Indian will eventually go after death. The spirits of those of an opposite temperament remain on this earth for an indefinite period. The latter are the mysterious spirits which the Indians call ghosts.

An important event in the life of an Indian is an eclipse of the sun. This obscuration is looked upon with terror by all tribesmen. As the phenomenon manifests itself, sacred incenses are burned in the lodges; holy men indulge in prayer; younger tribesmen pick up their firearms and shoot at the darkened orb in an effort to revive it, for according to their beliefs, the sun is dying.

I remember an eclipse of the sun which took place, years ago, when I was living with my parents on the Peigan Reserve. At the first sign of this phenomenon there was a great commotion in our camp. A number of warriors fired shots at the sun, others chanted sacred songs, while frightened women with their screaming children congregated in log shanties to have their faces painted with sacred paint by old men, as a protection against any evil which might result from the eclipse. A number of us children were dragged before my grandfather, Crow Flag—whose name I have inherited—to have our faces painted as a protection against any danger resulting from the eclipse. All over our reserve individuals could be seen shooting upwards to the sky, while others were deep in prayer during the short period of this remarkable event. Of course education of the Indians has done away with all this superstition in regard to an eclipse. We no longer waste good ammunition on this phenomenon, since we are now fully aware that a bullet cannot reach the sun.

An electric storm also played an important part in the beliefs of the original peoples of this country. A huge bird was supposed to be the cause of all the flashes of lightning and peals of thunder during an electric storm. The flashes were supposed to be the line of vision of this mysterious bird whose roaring we also heard.

Another of nature's phenomena to which we attached superstitious significance was the rainbow. We called it "Napi's lariat." I already mentioned Napi as an individual possessing supernatural powers. Indian history credits him with creating the world and all its inhabitants after a great deluge had devastated the former universe. Possessing this supernatural power, Napi also had control over various kinds of weather. The appearance of a rainbow during a shower was an indication that the storm would subside in a short time, for, in the words of the Indian belief, "Napi has lassoed the storm."

Many Indian children derived their names from the superstitious beliefs in regard to thunder. Such appellations as "Heard Everywhere" or "Heard Coming" were frequently used.

A large number of us Indians were travelling to a nearby city during the summer of 1910 to participate in the annual exhibition and pioneer celebration which was to be held there. At that time of year the rivers were usually flooded, causing great inconvenience to those who wished to cross to the other side. On this particular occasion we encountered a flooded ford, the foaming waters carrying with them trees and bushes uprooted from the banks. Before we dared venture into the flood one of our old men stood on its banks and intoned the following prayer:

Help us, dwellers of the waters. Hear my prayer.
Guide us every one in this company safely across

*this river. Let no harm come upon us while we
are crossing. With this request I offer you presents.*

At the conclusion of the prayer he discarded a bundle of old
clothes into the mud-swirling waters, and we were then allowed to proceed across. Needless to say every one arrived
safely on the other side.

Indians believe that all rivers are inhabited by water spirits
who are held to be the cause of some of the drownings that
occur. To appease these spirits the Indians ask for their protection and guidance while crossing a river. Presents consisting
of clothes and tobacco are also offered to these spirits by throwing them into the flooded waters.

CHAPTER ELEVEN

Hunting and Diet

I AM HAPPY to relate at the outset of this chapter that any information I give relative to the above subject is not derived second-hand. Furthermore, at times, my ire has been aroused to a high pitch when I read an article written by anyone who professes to have intimate knowledge of the habits of my people because oftentimes these literary contributions are entirely lacking in their authenticity. As an example, a retired police-man wrote an article recently claiming that Indians included snakes and other reptiles in their menus in the early days of western Canada.

The Blackfoot Indians are what I would call a carnivorous people, their main means of subsistence being meat, which was derived from the buffalo. These animals abounded on these vast Alberta prairies in countless thousands at that period of time.

There were two ways adopted by the Indian in despatching the buffalo. When following the first method, success depended upon numerical strength. This required the engaging of a large number of young men to participate in the hunt, which took place in the vicinity of one of the hundreds of natural "buffalo pounds" scattered throughout western Canada. These pounds were large, deep depressions in the ground at the foot of a steep bank. A runway or lane, cone-shaped, was constructed first, with large boulders on the flat at the top, in line with the depression at the bottom of the hill. These large rocks were placed at certain distances apart; behind each boulder a warrior concealed himself, armed with a robe. Mounted men previously detailed by the chief drove in a large herd of buffalo. As soon as the herd approached the first two boulders farthest from the bank, a member of the mounted warriors covered himself and his mount with a large buffalo hide and immediately galloped his horse to the head of the herd, for the purpose of decoying them through the lane of boulders. As the herd passed each boulder, the warriors crouching behind these huge rocks jumped to their feet and began shouting and yelling, accompanying this by waving their robes vigorously and extending their efforts by assisting the mounted men in driving the buffalo towards their doom, which was accomplished when they fell off the bank into the pound. Some of the animals were killed outright from the effects of the fall while others suffered broken legs and other injuries. The uninjured buffalo went round and round the inside of the pound while the warriors stood on the edge and shot them down with their arrows.

In this hazardous manner the primitive Indian acquired

Blood woman drying meat

his supply of fresh meat which was the chief item on his menu.

The second method followed in killing a buffalo was for a hunter to go and run a herd of buffalo and shoot one, bringing home the meat on another horse which he brought along for that purpose, for he never used his buffalo running horse for carrying meat.

After the meat was brought home by the hunter to his tepee, it was cut up into numerous long slabs by his women who were very skillful in this line of work. These slabs were then hung on wooden frames in the sun to dry. When the drying process was completed, the meat was mixed with wild mint for preserving purposes and packed away in skin bags for future use. By this method the meat retained its taste for an indefinite period and there was no chance of its going bad.

When the meat was ready for use, most women took a slab and roasted it over hot wood ashes; others took a slab, roasted it and pounded it fine, using a flat rock and a smaller one for hammering. To make it palatable, the ground meat was mixed with grease and saskatoon berries.

Another method followed in cooking fresh meat was somewhat similar to the procedure followed in "corn roasts." A stout stick, sharpened at both ends, was employed in cooking meat in this fashion. The stick was inserted deeply into the meat at one end, while the other end was stuck in the ground close to the fire. The meat was then turned at intervals until nicely cooked and ready for use.

A large amount of fresh meat was cooked by digging a hole in the ground roomy enough for the purpose. A layer of clean leaves was then placed at the bottom of the hole and the meat placed on top of the leaves, away from the sides of the hole. Another thick layer of leaves was then put on top of the meat, covering it entirely, and this in turn was covered with wet mud. A fire was built on top of the mud and in a little while the ashes, mud and leaves were taken away and a nice brown cooked roast was found all ready to serve.

Wild berries such as choke cherries, saskatoon berries, goose berries and bull berries, also provided an item on the Indian's menu. The choke cherries, which grow and ripen in abundance in July of each year were picked by our women, in skin bags, worn suspended on a cord around their necks. When a sufficient supply was picked, it was taken home and there it underwent a crushing treatment by a woman who sat beside her supply of choke cherries spread out on a robe, and with the aid of a large flat rock, and a smaller one for crushing purposes, pounds all her berries fine. Having completed her task, she next formed the crushed berries into small round cakes which she spread out on a robe in the sun until they were dry, when she packed them away for winter use. These choke cherry cakes were soaked and pounded again fine, and mixed with grease, before they could be eaten.

The saskatoon berries are more tasty and do not require any pounding. They were simply picked by our women and dried in the sun, when they were packed away in bags for winter use. Goose berries were not preserved because they soon wither away if not used soon after they are picked from the bushes. Bull berries are crimson in color and give their best flavor in the fall season, soon after the first frost of winter catches them. They are very hardy and can be preserved for future use.

Another minor natural product eaten by the Indian was a large root which we call the "prairie turnip"; it grows very abundantly in spots on the prairie. This wild turnip can be eaten raw or boiled and can also be roasted in hot ashes.

When spring time arrived, we children would repair to a nearby woods, select a tree, peel its bark off, and scrape off its sap. We used a piece of bark for a plate to hold the sap, which was very delicious.

Another natural food eaten by children was a certain kind of gumbo, very rarely found now. It is chiefly found on the banks and earth, and does not adhere to it when picked up.

This is the food the Blackfoot ate before the white man came to the prairies, and my people had a terrible time adjusting to the food which was brought to them by the white man. The Indians did not care for the meat of the domestic cattle; they claimed it was very offensive to the taste. When the Government of Canada signed a treaty with the Indians in 1877, rations of meat were given my people by the officials. When they vacated their camping place, huge pieces of meat were everywhere left behind by the Indians.

CHAPTER TWELVE

Origin of Indian Names
and Other Customs

I HAVE BEEN asked many times to explain the very curious names which Indians enjoy or otherwise support. There are three distinct types of name: the baby pet name, the hereditary name, and the war or battle name.

The pet names are used only by the parents, and by them only to their very young when they pick them up to fondle them. These names usually characterize some striking physical feature of the child. Hence, we often find such names as Pretty Girl or Pretty to Look At applied to the girl babies, and other names such as Small Boy among the male infants. Or a baby may not get a pet name; it may get its war name at birth. In choosing this name the parents will call in the assistance of an old warrior—one who is noted for his brave deeds on the field of battle. The warrior then recites his experience during open combat with the foe, and from these incidents the parents select a name. For instance, suppose that on one of his excursions he had killed two of his enemies, he would suggest Double Killer for a name. In the event of his having been shot at from both sides, Shot Both Sides would be suggested. Or, if he captured three rifles during a raid, Capture Three Guns. So he will continue until the parents have seized upon some name attractive to them. Then the old warrior takes the infant in his arms and prays that he may enjoy a long and happy life, finishing with the words: "I name this child Capture Three Guns (or any other name the parents have chosen). This accounts for the belligerent sounding titles many Indians possess.

The hereditary names are handed down from generation to generation and are usually considered strictly family property. The men may change their names at any time during their lives, but not so the women. When a male desires to change his name, he must find an ancestral one not in use, or else pay for one that is in use. I knew an old Indian who had four names during his lifetime, the first Red Leggings, the second Take Many Mules, the third Cow, and the final one Lynx Shield. The second of these was the only war name and originated in a feat of one of his relatives who once during a war raid had taken several mules from the enemy.

A few of the names have their origin in common, everyday occurrences. I knew a child with the queer name Ten Acres. On asking his parents for the origin of this name I was informed that the Indian Agency was very fond of the practice of selling just enough seed oats for ten acres to every Indian farmer, and since the words "ten acres" were on the lips of every reserve farmer applying for seed, the parents thought it would make a very suitable name.

Mountain Horse, the author's father, was a respected patriarch of the Blood tribe.

The original Indian Agency at Slideout served as the administrative headquarters for the Blood Reserve. It is seen here in 1890.

As friends of the Mounted Police, the Bloods sometimes held ceremonies at the barracks in Fort Macleod. Above, women participate in a dance in 1898.

Snake Woman, wife of treaty chief One Spot, was a member of the sacred *Motokix* society.

Rev. Samuel Trivett (3rd left rear) was the first missionary on the Blood Reserve. With him are Rev. J. W. Tims, Rev. George McKay, and Bloods at the Anglican mission in about 1885.

Girls in school uniforms march to class at the Anglican mission in about 1920.

Steel and his wife were both deeply involved in native religion and ceremonialism.

View of the Roman Catholic mission on the Blood Reserve near Standoff in 1910

Anglican mission on the Big Island, 1896. Left to right are the girls' dormitory, dining room and kitchen, rectory, three outbuildings, church, and boys' dormitory.

Tom Daly, Blood Indian, 1913

This painting is one of the few actual views of the Treaty Seven camp at Blackfoot Crossing in 1877. It was painted by Mounted Police surgeon R. B. Nevitt.

A tepee village was put up by the Bloods for the Lethbridge exhibition in about 1910.

Otter tepee on the Blood Reserve, 1892

An ancient method of carrying goods was the dog travois, seen here at Fort Macleod in 1916. It is held by Heavy Face, wife of White Calf.

Top—Missionary Calvin McQuesten attempts to secretly photograph a Pigeon Society ceremony at the Blood Sun Dance in 1907. *Middle*—His actions are seen by a member who rushes forward to order him away. *Bottom*—View of the Blood Sun Dance camp breaking up in 1893.

Woman with horse travois in Fort Macleod, late 1890s

Antelope tepee, Blood Reserve, 1892

The author, Mike Mountain Horse, in 1912

CHAPTER THIRTEEN

Civilization—Bad and Good

I SOMETIMES WONDER how long it will be before your so-called civilization extinguishes my people from the face of the earth. I am not, of course, speaking of those aspects of civilization so nobly exemplified by the missionaries and the North-West Mounted Police, but rather of the chicanery, drunkenness, greed and deception which made their appearance in conjunction with the finer phases of the white man's code, and which, as is usual with evil things, found so many willing pupils among my people.

Where are the tall, handsome, health, bronzed aborigines of yesterday? Most of them are in the Big Sands—the Indian settlement of the Hereafter, wherein all are welcome, good or bad; their earthly sins are forgiven and equal love is extended to all whose time on earth has expired. Surely a generous Heaven!

Where are the numberless thousands of Indians who once roamed the plains, valleys and mountains of this continent? Their hordes are now represented by a small and ever diminishing number of Indians.

The bad influence of the white race has affected the Indian both directly and indirectly. The worst of civilization, as introduced by the East, could but teach the Indian to swear, steal, drink and commit the many other crimes and atrocities which necessitate the criminal code of the white man. But indirectly, much disease and suffering, previously unknown, arrived with the "paleface."

Let us review the habits of the aborigine in so far as they affected his health. First, consider the Golden Rule of health preservation as taught in the schools and prescribed by the family physician: "Get plenty of fresh air. Sleep with the window open. Play outside. Walk, etc." The Indian lived the advice as to an outdoor existence. His home was a tepee with a large opening at the top for ventilation, an aperture which could not be closed. Sanitation in the nomadic days was no problem. At the least sign of accumulating filth of any kind, the dweller had merely to take down his dwelling and move to a location which had been cleansed by nature for countless years. His food consisted of buffalo meat, roots and wild berries. His susceptibility to colds and other ailments of the white man were unknown.

A party of warriors en route during very cold weather would often encounter a river frozen over, but with the ice not sufficiently strong to bear the weight of a man. One of the hardiest would be selected to cross the river first. This man would carry his clothing above his head, swim the icy river, and with his flint build a fire on the far bank. On his signal the whole party would swim across, dry their clothing, warm their bodies around the fire, and proceed on their journey, probably through considerable snow. But none of them ever became the victim of pneumonia—not even the sniffle of a cold in the head would be discernable as the result of an experience which would probably kill at least half the party of a similar number of the red men today.

It is therefore apparent that the early Indian's open air life, his staple foods, and his constant exercise, built up for him a constitution able to withstand any strain and hardship imposed on it during the time of a natural life span. By accident, old age, death in battle or clan feud, the early Indian made his trip to the Big Sands, but seldom through the sicknesses which ravage the tribes today and which were introduced by contact with the white man.

The diminishing ruggedness of the present day "educated" or "civilized" Indian is due to his lack of knowledge in adapting to the too-sudden change of habitation, food, and style of living introduced by the white man. It is to this class of Indian that I belong, and I speak from personal experience.

When the Federal administration which looks after the needs of the Indians first negotiated the famous treaty of 1877, one of its stipulations was that the Bloods and other tribes were to live on reserves under the supervision of officials appointed by the government. They went on these reserves and their early homes were built by them under the supervision of officials, who apparently had not considered the matter of reconciling the new with the old. These homes generally were rude log shacks containing one or more windows that could not be opened, and no ventilation other than the door. Tents were substituted in many cases, and these also had but one means of ventilation—the door flap. The tepee dweller was used to a perpetual movement of fresh air from the doorway up through the top opening. In the log shacks, the circulation of air was completely stopped, and in the tents it was diminished.

Needless to say, the war parties set forth no more; hunting was greatly decreased, the outdoor life diminished accordingly, and the Indians lived their fresh air existence less and less. This I believe to be one of the chief reasons why the Indian became so extremely susceptible to tuberculosis, and why that terrible disease became so prevalent among my people.

The old hardy diet of the Indians was perforce cast aside and food which they had previously never eaten was given or sold to them. Decaying teeth became known to the Indians for the first time, with all the resulting ailments. I have met Indians barely past middle age, with all their teeth gone—a "civilized" and unpleasant experience unknown prior to their change of diet.

The adaptation of the reserve Indian to his settled life, to the understanding of the sanitation that life demanded, to the ventilation of his new home, to the proper balance of ingredients in his new diet, was all too slow to meet the rapid changes which were forced upon him. The loss of a free and roaming life cost me and my people a very high price.

The last and most deplorable cause of the diminution of the Indian population is their fusion with the white race. To quote the words of an Indian: "Let the two races keep within the bounds of their own pastures!" My people are becoming extinguished rapidly enough without an unprofitable and miserable fusion with another race. The very thought is abhorrent to the right-thinking men of either race, for who has yet discovered a truly happy union between white and red? The better white men do not marry Indian girls, and our higher class of female youth, through instruction in racial hygiene, have no desire to intermarry.

On the other hand, there is no doubt that the North-West Mounted Police have been considered by the Indians to be their greatest allies and protectors. A comparatively handful of brave men, this organization gained control of the entire north-west, cleared it of its worst characters, and made life there safer for all. Law and order were brought out of chaos only because the men who comprised the force were of sterling character, men who held their honor higher than the briber's gold and were willing to face quick death on the plains, or the slower finish on the trail in the frozen North, in the upholding of a traditional principle.

Perhaps the first and hardest task of the Mounties was fighting the whiskey traders and preventing these men from providing the Indians with "fire water," which always resulted in brawls and killings.

A close second in difficulty was the abolishment of tribal wars, which meant the end of the warrior—the highest calling in the eyes of the Indian male. Also, the Indians had to be discouraged in their business (for business it verily was) of stealing horses from ranchers and hereditary enemy tribes across the American line. To "run" a herd of stolen horses across the border in early days was considered by the Bloods as not only a profitable occupation, but a feat of gallantry and daring as well. For this reason it took much time and patience to persuade the Blackfoot Confederacy to desist from the practice and to settle down to a slower and much less honourable—in the Indian's opinion—business of horse-raising and agriculture.

Colonel James F. Macleod, beloved officer commanding the North-West Mounted Police, never broke his word to the Indians. He was an aggressive and bold leader who achieved results that went a long way toward making Canada the most law-abiding country of its size in the world. He was afraid of no one, and perhaps this was the secret of his success with the Indians, though he did not rule them entirely through fear. The Indians did not understand the white man's laws, did not want them, nor in many cases agree with them, but there was one quality which they did understand and appreciate to its fullest extent, and that was courage.

But even courage alone could not win the case for the Mounties. What really made the Red Man adopt principles and laws foreign to them was that these laws were administered with such bravery, fairness and honour on the part of the administrators that the respect of the Indians was completely won. These were qualities which the Indians loved, admired, and from their viewpoint, had always practised.

Shortly after the police and missionaries arrived, the Indians settled on reserves allotted to them by treaty, and it was then that the missionaries began to carry on their onerous tasks. Very difficult it was for them, for first they had to learn the Indian language. Only the white reader who has struggled his way through an Indian dialect will realize the difficulty of this. Secondly, they had to combat the various traditional practices prevalent among my people at the time. And lastly, they had to inculcate the principles of Christianity into the minds of the Indians.

Three stupendous tasks! The tedious learning of a language from persons who did not understand the questions asked of them; the overcoming of resentment in order to change old and unsanitary customs; the teaching of a religion revolving entirely on the belief in one God, to prospective converts who already were supplied with more deities than they knew how to propitiate! However, the teaching of the missionaries was of a practical nature. They quickly perceived that they had to improve the living conditions of the Indians before they could hope to accomplish anything toward raising their moral and spiritual status, and it is chiefly due to this practical outlook that their teachings were eventually accepted.

With the idea of setting the Indians firmly on their own feet industrially, farm instructors and agents were sent to the reserve by the government to teach them agriculture. Day schools were established where the Indian children were taught. Boys' homes and hospitals were erected on the various reserves.

The missionaries worked hard for the welfare of the Indians on all the reserves, and great moral changes have been wrought. A new era dawned, the old life quickly passing away, and the Indians began eagerly to look forward to still further advances through the aid of those who were so nobly striving to help them. Today green fields of grain may be seen stretching for miles across the various reserves.

In the early 1890s, the Bloods had only begun to adjust to the new mode of life brought to them by a foreign race. The clothing worn by men consisted of a shirt, a pair of leggings worn with a breech cloth, moccasins and a blanket. The women wore long loose dresses, wide leather belts studded with brass

The author (back row, fourth left) was captain of the soccer team at Calgary Indian Industrial School in 1905. Other Indians, in white shirts, are: back row, Robert Red Horn, Peigan; Percy Smith, Peigan; James Little Bear, Sarcee. Middle row, George Big Crow, Sarcee; James Gladstone, Blood; Jack Wolf Leg, Blackfoot. Front row, Ronald Hoof, Blood; Charles Crow Chief, Sarcee; Herbert White Owl; and Cecil Tallow, Blood.

tacks, and moccasins. For head covering a woman used a handkerchief. A blanket also completed her wardrobe. If pants were bought by an Indian, the legs were cut off and a breech cloth worn with them. If a hat were used its crown was cut away for the purpose of letting in the air. Boots of any description were never worn by either sex.

Sometimes a prominent head man would issue invitations to other leading men for a social evening. At these gatherings the usual custom was followed of smoking from a huge pipe passed around at intervals, and story telling. Occasionally the host would sit down to entertain his guests without his trousers on, but this was only when the tepee was too warm.

About the only industry among the Indians at that time was the raising of large pony herds, in which some succeeded very well. A few years later the Indian Department decided to try and encourage stock-raising by my people and a system of trading horses for cattle was introduced. This resulted in a number of Indians owning fair-sized herds of cattle which they sold to the Indian Department for rationing purposes. All monies derived from such sales were credited to the individual Indian at the agency. Wagons and farm implements then began to make their appearance among the Indians. Hay cutting time would see long lines of hay racks filled with hay moving in the direction of a nearby town. This hay was also sold for Mounted Police requirements at the various police detachments.

Considerable progress, too, was made by the different churches in persuading the Indians to change their faith. Numerous adults on our reserve were baptized and confirmed. Two from the Blackfoot Reserve actually stood up in a church pulpit several times and preached the Gospel message.

Schools were administered by different religious denominations. Pupils attended these schools up to the age of eighteen, when they were discharged and returned to the reserves. Some of these ex-pupils became successful in the lines which they studied at these educational institutions. I attended the Calgary Indian Industrial School, built exclusively for Indian boys from various reserves in Western Canada. This great educational centre taught its pupils carpentry, farming, printing and the bakery trade. These proved very useful to many of the students who graduated from that school.

In 1905, when I graduated, the Indians were still being fed by the government, with rations of flour and meat being issued to us twice a week. But since my people had proved to the Indian Department that they could be self-supporting, the system was abolished soon after. Rationing was then confined to older and invalided tribesmen.

Rubber-tired buggies and democrats were a common means of locomotion at this period, the travois having been discarded some years earlier. A few years later agricultural pursuits were encouraged by Department officials. Thousands of acres of land were sown to wheat and oats annually. Modern homes and community halls, replacing the primitive log structures which had served in the past, began to make their appearance. These were built entirely by Indians.

The attitude of my people during World War One is sufficient proof of their right to be called British subjects. I defy anyone to cite a single instance of an Indian serving as a conscript in that war. The Indian is a born warrior; it has always been the part of a brave to fight his enemies. Therefore, any legislation making it compulsory for a nation to fight a foreign foe would appear ludicrous in the eyes of the Indian.

Further proof of the progress of my people during the past sixty years may be given in the following facts: By the 1930s our women folk no longer served as servile drudges; every Sunday the churches on the various reserves were filled with well-dressed Indian couples who, in most cases, drove to worship in modern, up-to-date cars, some equipped with radios. Some of our young ladies were serving as qualified registered nurses in many of the hospitals throughout Canada.

It has been a hard struggle, I must admit, for those who have helped us in the past. Still, I think some credit is due my people for the advancement they have made. We are not looking forward to the time when the buffalo shall return. Nor are we anticipating a time when the white man shall disappear from the continent. But we are scanning the horizon for further chances of advancement and further opportunities of proving ourselves true and loyal subjects of the British Empire.

CHAPTER FOURTEEN

Legends

It is not my intention to relate a long series of fairy tales in this book. I merely wish to offer a few examples which reflect the beliefs of the Indians in regard to the elements. These ancient beliefs have been handed down from generation to generation, and while my people view them as authentic in origin, they do not hesitate to use them, as the white people use fairy tales, as a means of coaxing their young ones to sleep.

Legend of the Beginning

A long time ago there was a great flood. Water was everywhere and no living thing was there except one being called Napi, and a solitary muskrat. Napi said to the muskrat: "You must dive to the bottom of this water and bring up some earth." The muskrat accordingly dived but the distance to the bottom was so great that when he returned it was as a floating dead body. Upon examination, Napi discovered that he had reached the earth, for in his claws there was soil. Napi took this soil in his hands and commenced rolling it, and as he rolled the soil it multiplied and fell and blew and scattered from him until the present earth's surface was formed.

Having made the earth, Napi picked up some of the soil he had generated and formed animals and birds which, after giving them the breath of life, he freed to habitate the land and air.

Then, after long solitude, Napi realized his need of a human mate. Picking up more soil, he constructed the form of a woman, into which he breathed life. This woman became his constant companion and together they had much enjoyment in the ruling of the world.

One day, Napi and his woman were sitting by the river bank in deep meditation as to ways in which to improve the earth. Napi rose, picked a buffalo chip from the ground, and said to his companion: "I will cast this buffalo chip into the water. If it floats, I will cause the coming generations to rise again following their death."

But the woman restrained him, saying, "Not so, for by this means the earth would soon become over-populated. Rather, let me take this stone and cast it into the water. If it sinks, people will die for ever, but if it floats, life will be eternal." And so, through the woman's logic and influence (superior as it has proven even to this day) death came into the world as the Indian understands it.

After a time, owing to the heavy business of governing and arranging for the future of the world, Napi and the woman separated, and for many moons were not together. Napi, in order to carry on his projects, had created many men to help him. One day when he and his band were hunting for buffalo, Napi became separated from the rest and went alone as far as the Highwood River. Standing on the edge of the east bank, he observed below him in the valley a number of tepees, all of magnificent workmanship. Their chalky whiteness could be seen from afar, and the neatness and orderly fashion of the settlement greatly impressed him. He began to shout and wave to attract the attention of the owners. To his surprise he discovered that the inhabitants were the woman whom he had created and several woman companions who had been created by her. She came to meet him and explain her activities. Napi, deeply impressed by the resplendent encampment and the obvious advantage of having an amalgamation with the women who had made it, said: "I have created many men who are without women companions. Let us align my men on the bank of the river, and from them your women can select husbands." This the woman agreed to, and the men were accordingly aligned on the bank of the river, Napi standing with them.

Then the chief woman retired secretly and removed her

fine clothes. She unbraided and disarrayed her hair, donned dirty rags, and was the first of the women to go forth to choose a husband. Thus disguised she walked up to Napi and seizing his wrist announced her choice of him as a husband. Napi, however, seeing but an unkept hag and having in mind his own woman as mate, would not be led away. So the woman returned to her tepee alone. Gathering the others around her, she instructed them to go up to the bank and choose their husbands, but on no account was any of them to select Napi. The women did as directed; all chose husbands, and Napi was left standing on the bank alone. The chief woman again arrayed herself in her finery, combed and rearranged her hair, painted her face, and came forward to Napi. Shaking her fist at him she said, "You have made me ashamed in the eyes of all other women by not coming with me when I chose you for a husband. Now you will remain standing on that spot, but not as Napi, for I will prepare a charm which will turn you into a pine tree." And this huge pine tree is still to be seen standing in solitude somewhere along the banks of the Highwood River.

So runs the tribal legend of the formation of our earth, and of the subsequent development of its life.

Legend of the Moon
Long ago, a married woman had a lover. She was extremely enamoured of him and on frequent occasions indulged in clandestine trysts with him. Unable to meet him secretly any more because her husband's suspicions were aroused, she feigned illness for a period of four days which terminated in her supposed death. Her people laid her on a hillock, using a buffalo robe to cover her, and placing a pillow at her head. Large boulders placed on either side served to hold the robe down. This form of burial had been her special request during the last days of her illness.

"My relatives," she said, "when I die, do not bury me. Leave all my personal belongings beside me." The faker was left in this position by her mourning relatives. Later, her sorrowing husband returned for a last farewell. On arriving at the spot he found it vacant, because in the interim her paramour had visited her and both had taken flight.

A few days later her lover was seen at his camp accompanied by a young man whom nobody knew. In reality it was the woman disguised as a warrior. The child of the supposed dead woman, whose suspicions were also aroused because of the intense interest bestowed upon him by this strange young man, informed his father of his suspicions. "Father," he said, "I believe that man is my mother. Invariably he asks me to his side and fondles me. I recognize his voice as my mother's."

After thinking the matter over very carefully, the husband next day requested his aged mother to prepare a special soup. "I want to invite those two boys for supper," he told her. This soup was a great favourite with the wronged warrior's wife. It was made from the scrapings produced from tanning. In the process of tanning a buffalo skin, when the hide is bone dry it is scraped with an elk horn scraper. All shavings from these hides are boiled in an earthen pot and used as soup.

The two friends accepted the invitation. When his guests had seated themselves, the warrior recognized his wife. On being asked to partake of the soup, one of the boys refused, but the imposter accepted. Whereupon, the host jumped up and pointing an accusing finger at her denounced her for what she had done. "You shall die for your sins," he declared. "I have discovered your deception. You cannot disappear into the earth or climb to the sky for safety."

Her lover managed to escape but the woman was slower, and her husband had gained the entrance before she could flee. He pulled out his flint knife and she began to run to and fro before him. Realizing that her chances for escape were slim and that she could not save herself, she used supernatural powers which enabled her to float upward into space. As she was disappearing, her husband struck at her, severing one limb at the knee. The unfaithful one continued to float upward and at last planted herself on the moon. Today if you look at the moon when it is full you will observe the figure of a person with one leg, standing beside a fireplace.

Legend of the Big Dipper

The "Sevens" is a Blackfoot name for the Big Dipper.

There was once a certain warrior who was very fond of hunting. Occasionally, on his return home from these expeditions, he noticed traces of clay or dirt on his wife's face. This aroused his suspicion that she was meeting someone during his absences. "I will obtain tangible proof," he thought.

The next day, pretending to go on a hunting trip, he returned without disclosing himself to his wife and observed her engaged in the task of tanning a hide. After a short while she laid it aside and going into her tepee, came out again with a flint axe and a rawhide rope. Her husband followed her into the nearby brush. Reaching her objective, an old hollow tree stump higher than a man, she struck it, whereupon a serpent crawled out from the top and transformed itself into a handsome young man. The couple then began to make love, wrestling and rolling in the dirt; hence the traces of dirt on the woman's face which the husband had noticed on prior occasions.

The warrior waited until his wife had departed for home, when he also returned, only to pick up an earthen bowl and depart again. Arriving once more at the old stump he proceeded to tap on it with his knife, whereupon the reptile emerged from the top. With one tremendous blow the warrior cut its head off with his knife, and holding the bowl close to the headless body, let the blood drip into it until it was filled, when he returned to his lodge.

"Will you make some soup out of this buffalo blood?" he asked his wife. The woman complied and when the soup was ready she filled a bowl and offered it to her man. "Put it aside and let it cool," he said. "And you had better have some yourself." After his spouse had finished her portion he said to her: "You have drunk your sweetheart's blood."

Crow tepee, Blood Reserve, 1892. The seven circles in its ears represent the big dipper.

Wailing loudly for her lover, she repaired to the stump, only to see the headless body of the serpent hanging from the top, the blood still dripping therefrom. She returned to her tepee and yelled to her husband as she approached: "You will die too!" But he was waiting for her and chopped off her head with his axe before she could enter. The headless trunk he laid out for burial on one of the skins she had been tanning and went back to the main camp. "I am now bereaved," he told the headman. "My wife died of sickness while I was out hunting with her."

Her brothers, suspicious of her death, went out to the place and decided to remain there for an indefinite period. On their numerous hunting trips they usually left their youngest brother in charge of the camp. When they returned they frequently found that some stranger had been there and cooked their meals. One day while these brothers were in the tepee talking someone outside spoke to them in a wailing, lamenting voice. "Don't look out. I am your dead sister. My husband is responsible for my death. The knife he used you will see lying on the ground when you come out."

On another day the brothers again went hunting and as usual left the young boy to watch their camp. On this occasion the sister came in person to the boy. "I am appearing to you, my brother," she said, "because of the great affection I have always had for you."

The boy told the others of this incident and declared that he was afraid to be alone with the spirit of his sister.

"Hide yourself under the robe, and when she comes again, try to discover the source of her supernatural powers," they instructed him.

The boy did as he was advised and the sister again appeared at the camp. She was observed to pull out a buffalo robe, the border of which was partially ornamented with human scalps. The boy heard her say: "My six brothers' scalps will complete the border ornaments: my baby brother's scalp will complete the centre decoration."

This the boy recounted to his brothers. After further con-sultation the lad was advised to hide once more and steal her bag containing the ornamental robe and other belongings. The boy did as he was told and managed to steal a number of articles from her bag: a porcupine tail used by medicine men for doctoring; face paint; quills for decorative purposes; and buffalo sinews used for sewing. With these possessions the boys fled from the camp in fear of their sister's spirit.

On discovering her losses the sister immediately started

in pursuit. After travelling some distance, one of the runaways glanced behind and saw her approaching. "Look, there she is!" he cried to the others. She was gaining on them rapidly. "Throw away those porcupine quills, so she will lose time in picking them up," one of them suggested. The quills were thrown out and scattered to the wind. Thus more distance was covered. "There she is again," another cried as he observed her again appearing over the horizon. "Throw away the paint." This was done and the sister stopped to gather her paint off the ground. It enabled the boys to gain on her. "She's coming again," one of them panted as he observed her figure at a distance. "Scatter her thread." This was done, and after a while the porcupine tail was also discarded.

About this time the lads had reached a tree which they proceeded to climb, the oldest one at the bottom, the youngest at the top. Here their sister came upon them. "I am going to kill every one of you," she cried. She then climbed up and knocked down one after the other, until she reached the sixth brother. A bird then flew by and screeched out to the one occupying the highest perch, "Shoot that feather in her hair or else she will kill you, too." The lad took careful aim and letting fly an arrow, hit the feather, splitting it in twain. Whereupon the woman fell from the tree dead.

The lone survivor then descended from his perch and laid his brothers side by side on the ground. Taking his bow and arrows he shot upwards, calling out loudly as he did so, "Look out, my brothers! An arrow is coming down. It may hurt you. Jump up!" He repeated this performance four times. On the fourth, his brothers responded by jumping to their feet.

A consultation was then held as to their next procedure. Some advised returning to the camp, but the youngest said: "No. Our sister is supernatural. She may rise again and kill us. Let us ascend to the skies and form a part of the stars." They stood in the form of a dipper. "Now shut your eyes and don't open them until I give the word," the boy told them. They followed his instructions. Upon the word being given, they opened their eyes and found themselves in the skies, still standing in the form of a dipper.

Legend of Medicine Rock

In the days when countless herds of buffalo roamed the prairies, the Blood tribe once made their winter quarters along the St. Mary river bottom, in the vicinity of the present city of Lethbridge.

One day an Indian in quest of the bearded monarch of the

plains stood on top of the knoll above the later site of Ashcroft Mine. Looking across the river he observed someone walking toward it from one of the neighboring knolls south of what became Brewery Road. Wondering who it could be, he turned north and coming within the vicinity of the present CPR high level bridge, descended to the river. On his way across he looked again and saw the same person standing on the edge of the knoll, apparently in quest of something. On closer observation he could see that he was a Medicine Pipe man. Such a man always dyes his blanket or robe a dark red; he also wears a tuft of hair in a little knot, about three or four inches long, on top of his forehead, and his face and hair are painted red as an insignia of his position.

This fellow was finally observed by the warrior to descend the hill and make for the river bottom. On reaching the foot of the hill, he squatted down, Indian fashion. The hunter, riding up to the site, was surprised to discover nothing but a solid, reddish rock, resembling a man in sitting posture. He then ascended the hill and looked in all directions, but failed to find any living person. He again descended and offered prayers in close proximity to the rock. The following night a stranger appeared to the hunter in a dream: "My son," he said, "I am the rock you saw. I want you and your children to come and make offerings to me at all times."

From that time on this rock was known as Medicine Rock and was usually laden with gifts such as wearing apparel, tobacco, and food. In later years, the custom of offering these gifts ceased and the rock was eventually covered with dirt and coal slack.

CHAPTER FIFTEEN

Charcoal, and How He Grew Blacker

IN THE EIGHTH of the white man's Decalogue we are told, "Thou shalt not kill." No qualifications or conditions which the rule may vary are mentioned, and it was through running afoul of this commandment that the hero—or villain—of this narrative became famous—or infamous.

In the early days of the white man's advent, my people were instructed, under the white law, that whosoever killed a fellow being would be forced to pay for his crime by hanging on the scaffold. This was thoroughly inculcated into their minds, and while we now know that leniency is occasionally provided for under 'extenuating circumstances,' the Indians at that time were entirely unaware of such a possibility.

Charcoal, a Blood Indian of temperamental disposition, discovered that on several occasions his wife had held illicit trysts with a young brave of the reserve. He repeatedly warned this lover to withdraw his attentions, but without success, and finally a crisis was reached wherein Charcoal had either to act or lose his honour among his people.

Considerable tirade and calumny have been hurled at my people and at Charcoal for the ensuing events, but it seems to me entirely wrong that the tribe should be condemned from an unadvised viewpoint, or that even Charcoal should be

Charcoal

branded as a criminal and degenerate by those who knew little or nothing of his attitude in the matter. True, his ignorance of the law led him to such desperation that he subsequently killed a police officer, still I think it only fair that the reader should at least have the facts correctly presented to him before forming his own judgment.

The Charcoal case was intermittently on the front pages of the press for more than seven months. Most of the accounts written at the time were inaccurate, because those probing the crime were not in a position to divulge the facts for which a curious public was clamouring. Through my own study of the case, and the information I have gathered at first hand from those who were most familiar with it, I believe I have the first strictly accurate story of this Indian murder case. Here I wish to state emphatically that I have nothing other than the utmost respect for the Mounted Police, with whom I have had the pleasure of working on several occasions. But while past records of the Charcoal episode have been full of praise for the courage and audacity of the police, there is a distinctly ludicrous vein running through the whole affair, climaxing in the capture of Charcoal.

It was haying time on the Blood Reserve in the year 1896. Contracts called for large amounts of hay to be delivered by the Indians to any of the following points: main agency on the reserve; North-West Mounted Police detachments at Stand-off, Kipp, Macleod "D" Division headquarters, and Lethbridge "K" Division headquarters. Large numbers of Indians were camped north-east of Hillspring on the southern border of the Blood Reserve. This special haying camp was under the supervision of Cliff Clark, farm instructor of the reserve at that time, and Charcoal was one of those working at this camp.

One morning Charcoal asked his wife to accompany him and assist in the hay field. "I am not well this morning, I don't want to go," Pretty Kangaroo Woman replied, and was accordingly excused by her husband.

Charcoal came home from work unexpectedly that day and found his wife entertaining, in a fashion too hospitable even for an Indian hostess, a young man who was one of her distant relatives. Charcoal admonished his wife's paramour in somewhat the following words:

"Young man, listen to me. My wife is your relative. Discontinue these meetings and don't gossip. This will be a secret between the three of us. I have no inclination to let people know that I discovered you two. They would have a very poor opinion of me if they knew. So I will do nothing further."

The illicit lovers, however, were very enamoured of each other and refused to heed this warning. The young again had the temerity to intrude on Charcoal's household, to be discovered again. No second warning was issued by the wronged husband. The Indian prides himself on his stoicism and ability to conceal his emotions at all times. Thus Charcoal managed to hide his feelings.

One morning, shortly after the second episode, Charcoal again requested his wife to accompany him to the fields. "Come with me and tramp the hay down in the rack as I pitch it up," he said.

"I have a severe headache," his wife replied. "I do not think I can go."

With his suspicions aroused, Charcoal went to his labours alone and, hitching his team to his mower, commenced cutting hay. About a quarter of a mile away he observed the rival for his wife's affections engaged in the task of raking hay. He kept an eagle eye on him and his suspicions were augmented when the watched one made a sudden disappearance.

The suspense was too great for Charcoal to bear. He had arrived at the extremity of his endurance, his pride was stabbed to the quick, his soul was in torment. And if his heart flamed with murderous hate, who shall say that this condition, under similar circumstances, could have existed only in an Indian's breast?

Believing that the young man was once more visiting his wife, he decided that he would definitely and finally ascertain just what was going on. To unhitch his team and make his way home was but the work of a few minutes. On his arrival at his tepee he was informed that his wife had repaired to the river bottom to fetch wood. With still greater ire and jealousy— for he remembered the "severe headache" of the morning— Charcoal armed himself with a rifle and rode to the river bottom. In a clearing by the bushes he spied his wife's horse grazing about unattended. Further on was another horse bridled with a harness bridle, also grazing, unattended. Proceeding through the surrounding brush in search of his wife, his face contorted with vicious purpose, Charcoal came to a half-built log stable. Peering through the apertures between the logs he discovered his wife in sinful tryst with her lover. Without any preamble, Charcoal shot through the chinks of the log structure at the invader of his domestic felicity. Severely wounded in the head, one of his eyeballs hanging from its socket, the young man sprang with the swiftness of a rattler to attack Charcoal. Fighting like maniacs, alternately beating each other down, falling under the rising again to deliver savage blows, the fight continued. The younger had the advantage of youth and strength, but this was more than offset by his terrible wound, and Charcoal, spurred on by mad fury, finally managed to beat his adversary into complete insensibility, when he was left for dead.

Next morning, two women meeting at the scene of the late conflict, heard moans coming from the log structure and their investigation disclosed a man lying on the ground inside. "Tell my brother to come for me," he said. "I am wounded. Charcoal is the man who shot me."

But the message as given was never delivered, for Charcoal, either hearing or surmising that his work was incomplete, returned and finally dispatched his enemy.

Police patrols and Indians, visiting the scene of the conflict later, found signs of a bloody struggle. Their visit took place following the discovery of the corpse by an Indian catching horses in close proximity to the log stable, and his reporting his gruesome find. It was decided by the police that this was a clear case of first degree murder and immediate steps were taken to apprehend the killer.

Strangely enough, Charcoal did not fall under suspicion during the early part of the investigation. Another Indian, Eagle Shoe, who, it was discovered, had had a quarrel with the slain man, was the first to be suspected. Charcoal, however, anticipating discovery sooner or later, and apparently giving way to desperation, was the first to strike. Making a nocturnal visit to the home of Mr. McNeil, a former employee on the reserve, he shot through a window, wounding McNeil in the side. Only the deflection of the bullet by a flower pot at the time of shooting, and the later administrations of Robert Wilson, whose rudimentary knowledge of surgery enabled him to cleanse and dress the wound, saved McNeil's life. But this was only one of the many visits and escapades made by Charcoal from his hiding places in the days following his flight from justice.

For instead of appearing before the police and attempting to vindicate his action, or going to the Indian Agent and letting him hear his story, Charcoal had sought refuge in flight. Six persons accompanied him, his two wives—Pretty Kangaroo Woman and Sleeping Woman—one of his wives' mothers, his grown daughter, and two boys.

Pitching their tent in close proximity to Chief Mountain, Charcoal made many nightly excursions to the surrounding country in quest of food and other commodities. Once he visited the Mounted Police detachment at Cardston and appropriated some of the officers' equipment—I believe it was Inspector Davidson's. On this occasion he was surprised during his raid and took cover behind a watering trough, where Sergeant Armor approached, a lantern in hand, to water his horse. Charcoal fired at the officer, grazing him, and the sergeant promptly retreated to a less valorous, but much safer, position.

One morning, in a frenzy of despair, Charcoal walked to the top of a hill near his tepee, and gazing out over the Belly Buttes, the scene of his boyhood days, he sang his battle song. Then, thinking of friends, old associates, old customs, and his life prior to becoming a fugitive, he wept aloud, his family witnessing his anguish. What terrible suffering, what torture his soul must have undergone, as he looked down at the ter-. ritory where he had always known liberty, respect, and never fear. These tribulations will never be appreciated by either myself or the reader, who has not thoroughly known the red man's wandering and free existence and his comparatively happy life on the Blood Reserve.

On his return to his tent, his daughter, seeing the tear stains on his face, wept also. "My father," she sobbed, "I wish that I might kill her," indicating her step-mother, the faithless wife of Charcoal. "She is the cause of all our misfortune. You have been a good husband to her, but she has never appreciated your kindness. Let me kill her."

Be it to Charcoal's credit that, even in his extremity, he would not listen to such talk. "My child," he said, "you must not talk so. I know what is going to happen to me. But you are still young. You must go on with your life."

Now snow had begun to fly, which made tracking a great deal easier, and police patrols and Indians trailing the refugees discovered the exact whereabouts of Charcoal's camp, noting the smoke from the fire. A depot was established by the pursuers. Men were left to care for the horses, and the main company went a tedious journey on foot through the timber, reaching the fugitive camp at break of day. Chief Scout Green Grass warned both police and Indians not to shoot until the tepee was surrounded, when a general attack was to be made at a given signal. No sooner had these instructions been given than Charcoal came forth from his tepee, his rifle in one hand, the other shading his eyes as he carefully scanned the wooden area that lay before him. Always on the alert, and sensing human presence, he stepped back into his lodge. The attackers concentrated a barrage of shots on the top of the dwelling and then, from the front, rushed their objective. They found that Charcoal, his two wives, and one of the boys, had escaped by a back way. The mother-in-law, the girl, and the other boy were caught and taken into custody.

Reports as to Charcoal's flight from this time on vary, but the one officially accepted by my people is as follows: He and his depleted family party made their way back to the Blood Reserve, where they stole two horses—presumably police mounts—which were subsequently found by the Peigan Indians at the river bottom, where the town of Brocket now stands.

Meanwhile, Charcoal continued to the timber limit of the Peigan Indians at the Porcupine Hills, and from this place of refuge made many stealthy trips to their reserve for food. On the occasions when he left his camp, he tied each of his wives to widely separated trees, being suspicious, and rightly so, that they were only too ready to effect their escape.

One night when raiding the Peigan encampment for the purpose of procuring a fresh mount, he was surprised during his selection of a horse by a resident brave, Coming Door, who asked "What are you doing? Are you Charcoal?" For a reply Charcoal fired at his discoverer but without registering a hit. The fire was returned but Charcoal also escaped unscathed, and by the time Coming Door and his friends had organized a pursuit party, darkness concealed the trail.

On a later nocturnal visit to the Peigan Reserve, his destination was the Old Agency, and Charcoal's small son accompanied him. Leaving the boy at the river bank with instructions to wait for him, Charcoal rode across the river. On the way he met two boys coming from the Old Agency, but having drawn up the hood which was attached to his blanket coth, they did not recognize him. In his own words, as he related the experiences of that night to other Indian prisoners in the Macleod guard room at a later date, "I went up to a hand game that was being played in a tepee and stood among a crowd of boys. No one recognized me. I looked into the tepee and saw a Kootenay Indian sitting there. I got ready to shoot him but remembered I had left the boy on the opposite bank of the river. This prevented me from firing."

When Charcoal returned to the place where he had left the

Charcoal's wife

boy, he found that he had escaped, or been captured. What had actually occurred was that the boy had gone to the home of Woodman, a Peigan Indian, who took him to the Mounted Police detachment located about a mile away. The police, interrogating the boy that night, were informed of the whereabouts of Charcoal's haunts in the Porcupine Hills.

Next morning, in company with Mounted Police and Indians, the boy directed the officers to his father's place of hiding. In the interim, the refugee had not been idle. Anticipating that the boy might bring the police to his camp, he moved his location northward about a mile, and, watching his previous site, saw the horses approaching it. "There is my son guiding the police to where we were camped," he called to his wives. Thus, once more, he was able to evade his pursuers.

As previously mentioned, whenever Charcoal left his hiding place in quest of food, he invariably tied his women to trees, far apart. One morning he omitted part of this procedure insofar as he only tied their hands behind their backs, their legs together, then left them, some distance apart, on the ground. Before taking his leave he informed Pretty Kangaroo Woman that he had decided to kill her when he returned. Sleeping Woman observed his departure and when he was some distance away cried to her sister in distress, "How has he tied you?" On being told, she suggested that they roll toward each other. This they did, with great difficulty, after which they contrived to loosen their bonds, Sleeping Woman first releasing Pretty Kangaroo Woman's hands by using her teeth on the cords, and Pretty Kangaroo then releasing her. The women had barely gained the protection of the encircling wood when Charcoal returned and discovered their escape. Going to the edge of the brush he called them, and while one expressed a desire to return, the other exhorted her not to do so. The two then made their way to the Blood Reserve and after days of hardship arrived there with terribly lacerated feet. They were made captive by Rides at the Door, a Blood Indian, who handed them over to his chief and the Indian Agent, who in turn committed them to the care of the Mounties.

And now the case narrowed down to the pursuit of a lone fugitive. One night, with more snow on the ground, Charcoal rode forth on a food-hunting expedition, choosing as a likely destination some Indian camps and houses on the north side of the river, just east of the Peigan Agency. Knocking on the door of Jack Spear's house, he cried "Whose house is this?"

There were numerous Indians in the house, gambling, but no one answered his call, for all were aware of his reputation of shooting on sight. Some leaped behind the big cast iron stove, others utilized an all-too-small table, and one generously proportioned elderly lady, tipping the scale at approximately 300 pounds, attempted vainly to do a disappearing act into the sideboard. Finally, one fellow, more intrepid than the others, ventured to answer Charcoal's question.

"Where does my friend Running Crow live?" came the second query.

"At the next house," came the reply, and the hiding places disgorged their relieved occupants as Charcoal rode off in the direction indicated.

On arrival at Running Crow's house, Charcoal, still sitting his horse, called out requesting that food and necessary commodities be given him. But Running Crow decided to prepare a trap for him. Stationing himself behind the stove, armed with a rifle, and his two wives, armed with axes, on either side of the door, he invited Charcoal to dismount and enter. Again the fugitive's sense of impending danger warned him, and taking a short cut, he jumped his mount over an old root cellar and fled. Immediately after, two Mounted Police arrived at the camp from the opposite direction and were informed that Charcoal had just left. Pursuit was delayed, however, until the following morning, when eight Indians took up the easily followed trail in the snow, and at the same time, Big Face Chief, a Peigan Indian, was dispatched to Pincher Creek to inform police there of the discovery and direction of flight of the wanted man.

Charcoal struck south, coming to a farm house into which he broke and stole some food. His trailers came upon him, in the act of making a fire in the vicinity of Chipman's Creek. On sighting the posse, Charcoal remounted and galloped off, his desperation now seeming to change to a hysterical joy of combat, for as he rode he sang his battle song, and the Peigans followed in hot pursuit. Many Chiefs shouted to him, "Come back, my friend. No harm is coming to you!" Charcoal pulled up and looked back. But his momentary confidence was dispelled when Coming Door, another of the trailers, screamed at him, "Charcoal, you are now going to find out that it does not pay to be foolish!" On hearing these bitter words the fugitive galloped off again.

Jack Spear, riding a gray horse, fastest and hardest of the mounts of all the Peigans, closed in on the fleeing criminal.

Charcoal merely turned and looked at him, and the look alone sufficed to make Spear draw up and retreat to a greater distance. Twice the grey drew near Charcoal, and twice Spear hauled into a retreat on Charcoal's turning in his seat to glare at the pursuer, though the glare turned to derisive mirth as the retreats were made.

Tail Feathers, noted scout of the NWMP, requested Spear to trade mounts with him. John Holloway, interpreter for the police, made the same request, but both were ignored by Spear, even though he well knew that their horses were exhausted and could not gain on the pursued. And to this day that grey horse of Jack Spear's is spoken of as "Runaway Grey" by the Peigan Indians. Some of the posse whose mounts were played out by the long race, held on the tails of the horses of the other scouts in order to keep in the running.

At this stage of the pursuit Charcoal turned and addressing the Indians begged them to keep away as he was not on the offensive against his own people. But Sergeant Wilde had just arrived from Pincher Creek with a fresh horse and, riding hard, rapidly overhauled Charcoal. I am not criticizing the action of this intrepid young officer when he chose such a suicidal course as to ride on the left side of the elusive one, but I believe better judgment could have been employed. As he came along-side, the sergeant shouted at Charcoal, asking his name and attempting to seize hold of the fleeing Indian. Twice Charcoal motioned him away, then, when he saw the officer could not be dissuaded, he shot him from his saddle, rode a small distance on, then came back and circled around the fallen figure, singing his war song. He then shot the body again, took the horse and ammunition of the vanquished and continued his flight, at the same time, in his frenzy, motioning the Indians to follow him, for his terrible deed had held them in their tracks.

But the horses of the scouts were entirely played out by now, and to follow Charcoal, mounted on a fresh horse, was out of the question. Scout Tail Feathers, his anger aroused at seeing his superior shot down, mounted the horse Charcoal had left and kept on his trail. The others took the body of Sergeant Wilde and conveyed it to the farmhouse of John Dipadore, a Frenchman who lived nearby, whence it was transported to Pincher Creek.

Many and varied are the reports that have been chronicled as to the final capture of Charcoal, but I believe the following is the correct disclosure of the actual facts of the event.

In his last wanderings Charcoal, as always seemed inevitable, rode back to the Blood Reserve to the home of his brother, Left Hand, who had previously promised the police that he would aid in effecting a capture. Knocking at the door, the fugitive asked that it be opened and that he be given food. Left Hand, recognizing his brother's voice, quietly directed his wives to assist in the capture, then, raising his voice, invited Charcoal in. After feeding him and giving him a smoke, doubtless thus to disarm suspicion, one of Left Hand's wives, a woman weighing nearly 300 pounds, sprang upon Charcoal at a signal from her husband and bore him to the floor. With Left Hand's help the captive was held down till the other wife had summoned other Indians who came and tied him fast. He was then placed on a bed and word of his capture was carried to the police. In the interval he attempted suicide by pricking an artery with an awl but his act was detected in time to prevent his bleeding to death. The police came and took the prisoner away to Macleod, where he was subsequently convicted of the murder of Sergeant Wilde and executed on the scaffold there in 1897.

For his part in effecting the capture of Charcoal Left Hand was officially awarded a chieftainship by the Department of Indian Affairs, but the Indians themselves never recognized his authority. In fact, they all adopted a particularly belligerent attitude toward him, believing his act to be unbrotherly in

Blood scouts at Standoff, 1894. Left to right: Calf Tail, Black Eagle, Big Rib, Many White Horses, Tailfeathers, Many Mules, and Meat Mouth.

the extreme. After the execution of Charcoal, a large number of Bloods congregated at the Catholic mission to pay their last respects. Following the ceremony, Gambler, a childhood friend of the deceased, approached Left Hand, and after hurling at him all the vile epithets he could think of, proceeded to thrash him thoroughly with his whip. Others were about to repeat the punishment but were stopped by timely intervention.

Thus ends the story of Charcoal, a wronged man bent on protecting his honour, and through ignorance of the law becoming more and more involved in deeds of desperation.

CHAPTER SIXTEEN

Tragedy at 18-Mile Lake

"Scout, GET DRESSED for the orderly room at 10 o'clock, the O.C. wishes to see you." I was given this order by the D.O., Corporal Wilson, at the Lethbridge Mounted Police barracks, in the fall of 1908. At 10 o'clock on that memorable morning I was paraded before the officer commanding, Supt. J. O. Wilson by Sergt. Major Raven. After surveying me with his official eye and consulting his subordinate the Sergt. Major, Mr. Wilson, a man beloved by my people for his fairness, ordered me to the Raymond area for duty.

"Mike, I have had you paraded before me this morning," he said, "to acquaint you of the fact that liquor is being sold to Indians in large quantities at Raymond. Now Corporal Wade has instructions as to your subsistence allowances. Proceed to Raymond at once and locate this source of supply. Use the phone whenever you need instruction or help, that is all."

"Left turn," said the Sergt. Major and I was ordered out, proud of the fact that an important mission had just been allotted me. I saddled my horse, Silver, and proceeded to Raymond. A strong moon was casting its rays over the small town as I rode up its deep rutted streets to the only feed stable in town. After giving instructions for my horse, I went to the restaurant of Quang Sang, a Chinese place patronized chiefly by Indians who were working in the sugar beet fields. Before entering this place, I heard loud altercations between two Indians who were about to engage in a fistic encounter. One of these would-be combatants, Two Guns by name, observing my entrance, started to make a quick exit by a rear entrance of the store. Quick action on my part was rewarded, for I collared this individual and found him to be very much under the effect of strong drink. I gleaned information from him that the proprietor had been selling "soft" drinks to Indians at 50¢ a drink that evening. I let him go to his tent, to hold himself in readiness when called upon.

Next morning, phoning in to Lethbridge for instructions, I was told to wait for police officials. In the interim I apprehended another Indian for being bibulous in this same Chinese eating place. I did not bother with the proprietor of this cafe, preferring to leave him for the police, although I had sufficient evidence to warrant his incarceration. About 11:30 a.m. Sergt. Major Raven, in company with Constable Mead, arrived by buckboard. We locked my first prisoner in the town jail. Good Strikes, my second prisoner, caused me considerable trouble by fighting in front of the Raymond Hotel when I went for him; it took the combined efforts of three policemen to put him in our buckboard. After we had our two prisoners under lock and key, a complaint was made by a local citizen against an Indian woman by the name of Susie Iron Pipe. This woman had indulged in the cup that cheers on a previous occasion to a considerable extent. I was sent out by Sergt. Major Raven to apprehend her and I located her at another Chinese place, still indisposed from her previous evening's merriment.

In the meantime, Mounted Police and Mr. Rodeback, town marshal, had raided Quang Sang's place, and seized a quantity of his supply of soft drinks which later under government analysis proved to be over 50 per cent spirits. We now had four prisoners on our hands, three Indians and the Chinese who had been arrested for supplying the intoxicants to our prisoners.

"Scout, I am going home by train at 5 p.m. today," said Sergt. Major Raven. "Constable Mead and you will convey the prisoners to Lethbridge by trail right away." We immediately departed with our prisoners. A few miles north of Raymond is a body of water known to hunters as the 18 Mile Lake, with the Lethbridge trail running on the east side of it. At the extreme north end of this lake, we observed a tent, with its door flaps blowing about in the wind. One of our prisoners, seeing this tent remarked, "Someone camping over there, digging potatoes, I suppose," not one of us realizing a horrible crime had been committed in close proximity to the tent. We arrived in Lethbridge and reported our prisoners to the barracks.

Now I will enter upon the second stage of this story, and in narrating it, I have not derived my information second hand because I accompanied police officials who went out to investigate this brutal murder.

New Robe, a Peigan Indian from Brocket, and his wife, Barking Dog, with their boy of 14 years of age, left the Peigan Reserve in the fall of 1908, for the purpose of seeking work in the beet fields around Raymond. Coming by way of Macleod, this man and his family stopped off at Lethbridge and made the acquaintance of a half-breed of the lowest type. I cannot describe the depth of this man's degeneracy; also he was an inveterate jailbird and a poltroon. I knew this character through having had to escort him at his work on numerous occasions during his incarceration at the guard room in Lethbridge. The half-breed, after loading up these Indians with liquor, asked permission to join them, which was granted. They then started for Raymond and pitched their tent at the north end of 18 Mile Lake, where whiskey drinking was indulged in to a considerable extent.

Imagine my surprise and indignation after reporting to the guard room and registering my prisoners from Raymond to hear a knock at my door, and hear the D.O. shouting, "Mike report to the Sergt. Major right away." I immediately paraded before that official.

"Get ready to come with me in 10 minutes, scout; never mind waiting for supper. Paul the cook will have lunch ready for us to eat on the road. Constable Wray is hitching up the team, and you will saddle up Spiny for your use. Take Rex with you and tie him on the buckboard." Rex was the Sergt. Major's bloodhound.

In about 10 minutes in company with the police officer, we proceeded on the Raymond trail. I wondering what on earth was taking us out at this ungodly hour, as darkness had already overtaken us. When we had left Lethbridge, with its lights far behind us, this officer turned and queried me.

"Scout, do you know what Indians are camping at the north end of 18 Mile Lake?"

"No sir, but I saw a tent there today when we passed by with the prisoners," I replied.

"Well, there are said to be some dead Indians at that tent," was his next information. I started to work on the theory that any Indians who may be at this tent had died from sickness and had been left at this place temporarily by their friends, before being taken back to the reserve for burial. Murder was obscure in my mind. It was far into the night when we made our way to the scene of the gruesome tragedy, driving up to the tent, after locating it by the light of its canvas.

"Hello there," our intrepid officer hollered. Getting no reply from within, he hollered again; still no reply. Climbing down from the buckboard, he walked into the tent to investigate, but came right out again.

"Mike, no one is in this tent," he informed me. "Get down from your horse and help me look around." As I jumped from my horse a sort of creepy feeling started going up and down my spine. First thing did in the dark was to kick a lantern.

"I have a lantern sir," I informed my superior.

"Good, come over here with it, my boy, and I will light it," was his reply. After we had lighted the lantern its first ray of light revealed a horrible scene to be long remembered by me. It revealed a man lying on his back, left leg straight out, right one bent at the knee, the trunk and head covered with a blanket. Sergt. Major Raven started pulling the coverings off this corpse.

"Do you know this fellow, Mike?" he asked me.

"No sir," I replied.

I gazed on the most horribly mutilated features I ever did see. The head of this corpse rested in a gore of blood, with half of its face shot away. A cold sweat broke out on me, as I started to back away from this gruesome sight. Imagine my fright, when I fell and landed square on top of another corpse in the dark. This was covered with a Hudson's Bay four-point blanket. I called out to the officer, "Here is another," as I regained my feet. He immediately came over with the lantern and discovered the corpse of a woman in the position of a Mohammedan at prayer. This corpse was minus the back of its head, bits of her brain and blood being scattered about in the grass.

"She is a total stranger to me, sir," I informed the policeman. As I started to walk away, I came across a fur robe spread out on the north side of the two corpses and parallel with the tent. I kicked at this robe only to find another body underneath it.

"I have one here, sir," I shouted to the officer, who came over with his lantern, pulling the fur robe off, he discovered a small boy about 14 years of age, with a big gaping wound in the right eye. Powder marks were pronounced around the edge of this wound. It was then that I found my first clue as to where these people came from. This poor boy had the customary long braids of an Indian. Closer scrutiny of his moccasins revealed the beadwork to be a pattern used only by the North Peigans at Brocket. It is called "Old Man's beadwork." I notified the official to this effect.

Talk about a scared Indian! I sure was one, with three murdered people lying around me and the possibility of their murderer lurking around in the dark, waiting to add me to his victims. However, I managed to put up a bold front to my superior.

"Mike," he said, "you had better stay here all night and guard this place. The O.C. and I will be out the first thing in the morning so don't let anyone touch anything around here."

"Yes, sir," I replied.

The Sergt. Major started to drive away, with my saddle horse tied to his team, but on the spur of the moment I sprinted after him and jumped into the buckboard. Realizing how frightened I was, he excused my action with the remark, "I guess you had better come in."

Next morning after a few hours' rest, Supt. J. O. Wilson, Sergt. Major Raven and I visited the scene of this horrible crime. Whiskey bottles were very much in evidence. I also noted that the pickets used for the tent were from pine trees, indicating that these Indians had lived in close proximity to the mountains. However, investigations by police officials failed to point the finger of suspicion to anyone. Hundreds of Indians visited the place, but none was able to identify the dead. Telegrams were sent to Indian reserves, asking for any missing persons, but without success.

Right after the discovery, I was sent to a farm for a young lady photographer, as Raymond did not boast of a photographer of its own. This young lady, Miss A. Collett, was reluctant to go with me, but on the assurance that I was a police interpreter, her people consented to let me escort her, but made me promise that I would bring her back safely. Miss Collett took a picture of the dead trio in a sitting position; also another photo of the whole sordid scene. After she had finished, I rode into Raymond with her, seeing her safely back to her grandmother's place. Riding up the street, I met Robert N. Wilson, who was Indian agent for the Blood Reserve.

"Hello, Mike, have you made your home here?" he greeted me.

"No, sir, I am out at 18 Mile Lake with the police, who are investigating a triple murder of three Indians. So far, no one has been able to identify them."

"Good lands! I wonder if New Robe did it? He left the Peigan reserve with his boy of 14 and his wife. Now he has returned alone and committed suicide."

I thanked the Indian Department official for this valuable information and immediately started back to acquaint the police of this news. I then received an order from the O.C. for the sergt. major to have the bodies and their effects taken into Lethbridge; this was done by three teams. Next time I saw these bodies they were lying in the undertaker's at Lethbridge. I do not know what disposition was made of them, or which gentlemen sat on the coroner's jury. A number of theories about the killings were formed, but the one which seems to be near the truth was this:

After these people had pitched their tent, the half-breed, under the influence of strong drink, started to be very amorous to the Indian's wife. New Robe showed his objections very strongly by engaging the half-breed in a fistic encounter, getting the worst of the battle. The half-breed then picked up a shotgun. New Robe, observing this, asked his boy to run for safety, but the half-breed, firing at random, shot the lad in the eye. New Robe, in a frenzy of rage at seeing his boy shot down, jumped on the half-breed, disarmed him, and shot him in the face. Meanwhile, the woman, seeing murder done, fell on her knees and begged for mercy from her husband, who replied, "You are the cause of all this," at the same time shooting her in the back of the head.

As the conclusion of this story, I would like to point out that these are the kinds of consequences which can result from supplying liquor to my people. From my own experience, when a number of Indians congregate to have an illicit drinking party, there is almost sure to be a fight. And they will keep on drinking until they are unable to control their normal facilities. So do not help to contaminate my people; don't try to be friendly by supplying us with bottles of strong drink. Instead, make it a point to help the Indian, so he can help himself.

CHAPTER SEVENTEEN

Our Warriors Die

IN THE SPRING of 1910 I was called to the bedside of my dying uncle, Chief Bull Shield. His capacious tepee was erected on a large flat in his allotment on our reserve and I noticed as I approached that my relatives had already congregated there with a number of other Indians, friends of the Bull Shield family. The chanting of a medicine man, accompanied by the steady beating of tom toms, could be distinctly heard from within the tepee as I approached with Arthur Bull Shields, one of my cousins. With utmost reverence we entered and seated ourselves on a robe near the door. As I gazed around the interior, I noticed that the last tribal rites of our people had already been performed by our immediate relatives.

My uncle lay in a state of coma on a bed of expensive colored shawls, breathing hard and coughing at long intervals. Dressed in a beautiful buckskin suit with ermine tails for fringes, his feet encased in snow-white beaded moccasins, he was all ready for that long journey to the Big Sand Hills—the Indian Here-er. My father, Mountain Horse, sat near his pillow brushing the flies away from his brother's face, using a hawk's wing as a fan. My aunt, Pipe Woman, sat near his feet shedding silent tears. Powdered red paint, I noticed, was sprinkled on the ground in the interior, half-way around, while blue powder completed the circle. Over this powdered paint, red and blue plumes were scattered. All these were insignia of the office held by my uncle in our tribe as an affluent and prominent chieftain. He was recorded as having the largest horse herd on our reserve, their number running into the thousands. He had had a colourful career, and the heroic achievements credited to him are worthy of an epic poem.

Surrounded by his sorrowing family and relatives, and amidst loud and hysterical weeping from those in attendance, this great chieftain passed to the "Great Beyond."

Four years after this sad episode, Great Britain was forced to declare hostilities on the Central Powers of Europe, and Canada immediately offered her assistance to the Mother Country. Canadians, regardless of religion or creed, rallied to the colors. From all parts of the Dominion they came, some travelling a considerable distance on foot. The intrepid sons of great warriors of various Indian tribes manifested their belief in the cause of the Great White Father by spontaneously enlisting in the Canadian Expeditionary Force. Some 3,500 Indian lads from all parts of Canada rallied to the colors in those hectic days. And although the proportion of the aborigine was in the minority, the power of their example was strong, and they were particularly mentioned by the Germans as enemies worthy of their opprobrium. Doubtless they had previously conceived a wholesome fear of the Indians whom they pictured in war paint, armed with tomahawks and scalping knives.

From the outset of this colossal struggle the Red Man demonstrated his loyalty to the British Crown in a very convincing manner. Patriotic and other war funds were generously subscribed to, and various lines of war work participated in at home. The Indian was not subject to the compulsory Military Act passed in 1917. Certain treaties with the Great White Father stipulated that they would lay down their weapons of war and fight no more. Therefore, any participation the Red Man had in the struggle of 1914 was one hundred per cent voluntary.

Many a wooden cross, marking the Red Man's sacrifice in the cause of civilization, may be seen in the military cemeteries throughout France. Susceptibility to tuberculosis also played havoc with our Indian fighters. Contracted in the trenches, due to cold and exposure, many died from this deadly disease on their return from the war. My own brother, Albert Mountain Horse, was one of these. Albert volunteered at the

Mike Mountain Horse (front row right) was a recruit in the 191st Battalion during World War One. Others in the group, left to right, back row: George Coming Singer, Joe Crow Chief, Dave Mills, George Strangling Wolf, and unknown; Front row: Nick King, Harold Chief Moon, Sgt. Maj. Bryan, and Joe Mountain Horse.

commencement of the war to see service with the First Canadian Expeditionary Force. Badly gassed three times, this young officer—for he was only 22 years of age—contracted consumption and was invalided home in November, 1915, dying at Quebec on his way. At the request of my father, the federal government shipped Albert's body from Quebec to Macleod, and a military funeral of note, largely attended by Indians and white men, was held in this pioneer town. It was conducted in the Indian tongue by that renowned pioneer missionary to the Indians, Archdeacon J. W. Tims of Calgary, assisted by the Rev. S. H. Middleton, Albert's school teacher and tutor. The Last Post was blown by Cadet Reggie Mountain Horse, and final interment was made at St. Paul's school cemetery. Thus the Blood tribe, a branch of the Blackfoot Indian confederacy, sacrificed the first of her sons to the cause of civilization.

Reared in the environment of my forefathers, the spirit of revenge for my brother's death manifested itself strongly in me as I gazed down on Albert lying in his coffin that cold winter day in November 1915. Soon after the funeral I obtained

indefinite leave from my work as an interpeter and scout for
the Royal North-West Mounted Police at Macleod, and with
my brother, Joe Mountain Horse and a number of other Indian
boys from neighboring reserves, I enlisted in the 191st Battalion
for service overseas.

Colonel W. C. Bryan was the recruiting officer at Macleod.

I can readily appreciate the easy adjustment of the white
man to the strict disciplinary measures of the army, but to
apply the same rules and regulations to young undisciplined
natives was quite another matter.

It was customary for new recruits to appear on parade two
or three times before they were issued uniforms. George Strangling Wolf, latest arrival in the battalion, appeared on parade
one morning wearing elk teeth earrings, with an elk teeth
necklace to match, and a gaudy red handkerchief around his
neck. The crown of his hat was cut away to let in the air, and
he was noisily chewing gum, much to the discomfort of the
man next to him in line. Thus he stood ready for inspection.

"What's your name?" was the first inkling I had that
George's ludicrous appearance had been noticed by the officer
in charge.

"George Strangling Wolf," murmured my friend.

"Well, Private Strangling Wolf, take this off, and this,
and this," said the officer, indicating with his cane the various
ornaments he wore. "And take that gum out of your mouth.
Next time you chew gum on parade you will get one week
sanitary fatigue. Private Mountain Horse, take this scarecrow
to the quarter masters and get him outfitted." After the officer
had addressed me, I walked off the parade grounds in company
with the so-called "scarecrow" amidst muffled giggles from
the other members of the awkward squad. Strangling Wolf,
however, turned out to be a very able soldier. He was badly
gassed at Lens in 1917, which caused him to be invalided home.

Another picturesque figure to don the uniform of the
Canadian Expeditionary Force was Bumble Bee. Although
unable to speak a word of English, he entered with an energetic
spirit into the period of training at Sarcee Camp, Military
District No. 13, near Calgary. Unfortunately, owing to the
belligerent attitude he maintained in regard to having his
hair cut (he still wore it long) he was struck off the strength
of our battalion. Before leaving for the reserve, Bumble Bee
admonished the rest of us in the following words:

"Don't be foolish like these white soldiers. I hear they
call the war off every day at mealtime. You boys want to keep

on shooting, even if you see them sitting down to eat."

Bumble Bee belonged to the old school. He was a son of Crow Chief whose two other boys, Nick and Joe, also enlisted for overseas service. Joe Crow Chief was wounded on the wrist in the allied offensive at Amiens in 1918. Nick was also a casualty at the Canal-de-nord, during the final retreat of Kaiser's soldiers.

Another new recruit to our battalion was a white man by the name of Kaiser. One morning, at roll call, when this unusual name was called, George Coming Singer, an Indian boy at the other end of the line, let his feelings get the better of him, and yelled out "That's the bird I'd like to get a shot at." Of course the officer could not let this pass. "Take this man's name and number" he demanded; the outcome of the incident was that I had to oversee George next day in the work of lugging huge latrine pails to the rear.

I will not burden the reader with further details of this period of training beyond stating that our boys were successful in adapting themselves to their new mode of life. After the necessary training in Canada and England, these descendants of mighty warriors gave a splendid account of themselves, both in the trenches and on the battlefields.

To realize the full horror of war, let the reader accompany me to the Vimy sector where I first underwent my baptism of fire. Lying on top of Vimy Ridge one night, along with a number of other Indian boys, the scene before our eyes might best be described as that of a huge stage with lighting effects— verry lights from the Hun lines, and flames from bursting shells in the city of Lens. The red glare thrown back appeared like a great fire in the sky all the time.

The trenches ran through almost to the heart of the French coal mining city. Here a brigade of the Germans had entrenched themselves so well that incessant bombardment by artillery and bombing from the air did not aid the boys from the Dominion to any great extent, although they had been in this sector for a long time. Along these miles of trenches one could see planes dropping bombs on the German lines, followed by geysers of smoke and dirt shooting skyward like volcanoes in eruption. One could witness houses bursting suddenly into flame as projectiles from heavy artillery of the enemy struck them. One could walk past Canadian howitzer batteries about a mile from the trenches in front and hear the 57 inch shells from these guns screaming overhead on their errands of death and destruction.

The war wave which swept into Lens had left awful evidence of its onslaught on this once peaceful city. As I listened one night to an enemy bomber droning like a huge bumble bee over the allied lines, the thought came to my mind, where is the God that the white man taught the Indian to believe in? Why does He allow this terrible destruction? And I prayed that He might yet bring the nations to their senses.

Amid these scenes of carnage and destruction the Indians held their own in the battles of the Empire. Some served as snipers and did exceedingly well as such. I should like to relate the achievements of four Indian lads who served in this branch of the C.E.F.

Philip McDonald, an Iroquois Indian of the 8th battalion, had 40 notches on the stock of his rifle when he was killed. The grandson of Louis Riel, of rebellion fame, had 38 officially observed hits when a bullet from an enemy sniper claimed his life. Ballendine, a western Indian, only survivor of this trio to return home to his family, is recorded officially as having sent 50 Huns to the Happy Hunting Grounds, at Warvillers, a small village in France captured by the 50th battalion of Calgary on the 18th of August 1918. Another Red man, Corporal Norwest, was shot through the head while endeavoring to locate a nest of enemy snipers. This young soldier was considered the greatest sniper in the B.E.F., officially recorded with 115 observed hits. Norwest used a special rifle fitted with telescopic sights, a present from one of the higher officials. He was awarded the Military Medal with bar. Corporal Norwest was an Indian from the vicinity of Edmonton who enlisted with the 50th battalion of Calgary.

Not only did the Indian excel in guerilla warfare, but many individual acts of bravery were credited to these sons of the plains. No more fitting theme for the pen of a romantic writer could be found than in the following accounts of bravery by Indian soldiers:

Joe Thunder enlisted with the 128th battalion and was transferred to the 50th battalion in France. One day he became separated from his platoon and was immediately converged on by six hefty "square heads." Joe bayoneted every one of them. He was awarded the Military Medal and in March 1918 was wounded most severely.

Another outstanding accomplishment by an Indian merited the award of the Distinguished Conduct Medal. George McLean alone dispatched 19 Germans with mills bombs, also capturing 14 more before he was wounded.

While the Red men were fighting the enemy on foreign soil, their people at home were doing their part by contributing to war funds and vigorously participating in various war activities. Women of the various reserves formed Red Cross societies and other patriotic associations, knitting warm socks, mufflers, and sweaters for the boys in the trenches, continuing their endeavors until the termination of the war. In buying Victory bonds the Indians also responded generously. Individual Indians sometimes invested huge sums, one chief alone buying $21,000 worth of Victory Bonds. The following figures comprise Canada's native people's contributions of $44,545.46 to various patriotic funds, including Red Cross, Belgian Relief Fund, Patriotic Funds, etc. during the war. By province, the contributions were: Ontario, $10,383.70; Quebec, $180; Manitoba, $3,019.60; Saskatchewan, $17,257.90; Alberta, $8,656.90; and British Columbia, $5,047.36.

My uncle, Chief Bull Shield, had been a great warrior of the plains. But the war proved that the fighting spirit of my tribe was not quelched through reservation life. When duty the plains. But the war in Europe proved that the fighting spirit of my tribe was not quelched through reservation life. When duty called, we were there and when we were called forth to fight for the cause of civilization, our people showed all the bravery of our warriors of old.

Index